The Deepest Revolution

William Randolph

Copyright 2025 William Randolph

Table of Contents

Words of Gratitude 1

Revolutionary Activities: This Book is Not Theoretical 2

Part 1 - This Is Who We Really Are 3
   Chapter 1: This Is Who We Really Are 4
   Chapter 2: Can Whole Nations Embrace Generosity and Integrity? .11
   Chapter 3: Healthy Nations Share Three Core Spiritual Practices . . .20
   Chapter 4: Imagine If Generosity Was Normal 28
   Chapter 5: Why Don't We All Live in Healthy Nations? 34

Part 2 - Why Are We So Lost 39
   Chapter 6: Why Are We So Lost? 40
   Chapter 7: Why Are People So Selfish? 49
   Chapter 8: Why Don't More People Stand Together? 58
   Chapter 9: Why Do People Obey Corrupt Leaders? 72
   Chapter 10: Why Are People So Racist and Hateful? 90
   Chapter 11: Can Whole Nations Embrace Awareness and Unity? .101
   Chapter 12: Selfish Violence vs Selfless Violence 106
   Chapter 13: Can Whole Nations Embrace High Standards? 114
   Chapter 14: This Pervasive Abuse Must End 130

Part 3 - The Deepest Revolution 143
   Chapter 15: The Biggest Secret in Human History 144
   Chapter 16: Build Your Spiritual Strength 150
   Chapter 17: Build a Healthy Nation One Community at a Time . .164
   Chapter 18: The Deepest Revolution 178

Glossary 181

Locations of Healthy Nations Referenced in this Book 183

Important Notes on Sensitive Topics 184

Copyright, Image Credits & Further Reading 186

Bibliography 187

Words of Gratitude

Thanks to all the nonhumans who helped me write this book. Thanks to the Carolina wrens who lifted my spirits in the morning, the wild dandelions and chickweed that nourished me, and the trees on the edge of a local clearcut logging operation who reminded me to stand strong in the face of terrible things.

I would not have known how to feel grateful for the nonhumans' gifts if it weren't for the Kamana program. Thanks to Jon Young and all the contributors who produced it.

Thank you to Mike Paul for your quick friendship and trust and inviting me to meet the Ashaninka. Thanks to the Ashaninka for showing me what a healthy nation is like.

I'm grateful to the people of healthy nations who interviewed or wrote about their traditional way of life, including Black Elk, Pretty Shield, Ohiyesa, Martín Prechtel, Nancy Basket, Robin Kimmerer, the unnamed authors of *Basic Call to Consciousness,* and the Zapatista writers.

And thanks to those who studied people of healthy nations and wrote about them respectfully, including Jean Liedloff, George Grinnell, Anne Cameron, and Frank Linderman.

Special thanks go to my editor Cindy Spitzer. I appreciated your patience as we worked and reworked the material. You supported my ambitious timelines and helped me change my writing style to make this as engaging as possible. I couldn't ask for a better editor. It has been a pleasure working with you.

Thank you to my early readers for holding this book to a high standard. Your feedback made a big difference.

Thanks to Bob, Seraina, Nina, Owen, Tod and Lindsey for your support.

Lastly, thanks to everyone who makes important information freely available online, including Internet Archive, Anna's Archive, Sci-Hub, ratical.org, and Wikileaks.

Revolutionary Activities: This Book is Not Theoretical

This book is about The Deepest Revolution. It explores what healthy nations are like where justice and mutual respect are pervasive, why unhealthy nations all have terrible troubles like corruption and greed that never go away, and how to create healthy communities and eventually new healthy nations.

But no one will give you a healthy nation to be part of. No one will hand you a beautiful way of life on a silver platter.

This book isn't about a "solution" – it's about a journey. I can't tell you every step needed to have a successful Deep Revolution, but I can tell you the kind of person you'd need to be to take part in it.

After studying many healthy nations and multiple Deep Revolutions, I noticed that in traditional times people in healthy nations all have certain things in common, such as deep connection with the Earth, integrity, bravery, joy, respect for children, deep awareness and mutual understanding, generosity, and gratitude. They have the spiritual strength to confront injustice, align their lives with the deepest truth, and live without shame. Each person gives their deepest love each moment as a normal way of life.

Sounds like a cool group of people to be around, right?

This book includes Revolutionary Activities meant to help you cultivate these qualities. I urge you to complete the activities. Let them challenge you. And don't just do each activity once, but do them repeatedly so they become a way of life. I know from experience that the more you work these activities, the deeper they will take you on a beautiful path of deep meaning and connection.

I believe that if you grew up in a healthy nation, many of these activities would be normal parts of your childhood training. But for people who didn't grow up this way, they'll train us to play a good part in the Deepest Revolution.

Part 1

This Is Who We Really Are

Chapter 1: This Is Who We Really Are

I have really good news!

If you're like most people (and like me until recently), you may think that troubles like racism, sexism, greed, and corruption are an intrinsic part of basic human nature, or inescapable aspects of every nation around the world.

The good news is this: it is possible to live without these troubles.

In fact, it's not just possible to live in a society without discrimination, selfishness, child abuse, and pollution; for millions of years this was the normal way for humans to live – and in some places, it still is.

I'm not talking about a weird cult or tiny communities of saints. I'm talking about hundreds of millions of people living in a beautiful way over millennia, all around the world, with no police, prisons, poverty, abuse, or hatred. Nations where sharing is a normal way of life, neighbors deeply trust each other, leaders serve the people, and visitors are treated like family.

Does this sound like a fantasy? I thought so too, until I was blessed to live briefly in such a place, a nation of thousands of people living across many villages deep in the Amazon forests.

My short time with the Ashaninka in 2015 was utterly magical and changed my life. An Englishman named Mike had been visiting the Ashaninka yearly for 35 years and respected them deeply, and when he saw that I would respect them too, he invited me to join him. He told me, "you will spend the rest of your life figuring out lessons to learn from these people."

Meet the Ashaninka

Before we entered Ashaninka territory, Mike said to expect exceptional generosity. But nothing prepared me for what I found. Everywhere I went, no matter what was happening, I was constantly offered food, drink, a place to rest, a chance to join their singing and dancing, and generally invited into their communities as if I weren't a strange white American man who didn't even speak their language. They just welcomed me without asking anything in return.

For example, whenever my host and I traveled around the region and needed to rest, we would stop at the next house and the hostess would bring us a fermented pink drink called peorentsi, along with some simple and filling food. They didn't do this because I was a special guest. Every traveler who needed to rest received food and drink with no expectation of trading or paying.

Dinners were likewise times of generous sharing, where people would bring the fish they'd caught, animals they'd hunted, and food they'd grown or found, and cook it up together over a fire in communal meals. No one counted who brought how much food, or who ate how much – people just shared, and every meal was fun. I never understood what they said unless my host translated to Spanish, but their joy and laughter were infectious.

Back in the United States, many people call work a "grind" or "rat race," but I never saw a single Ashaninka grinding, no matter what they were doing. One story really showed me how unstressful their work was: I once saw an older woman sitting outside on a mat, spinning cotton into yarn on a drop spindle. At first she sat upright, rhythmically working the spindle. After a while, she leaned over onto her elbow and worked from that relaxed position. Eventually, she leaned all the way over and took a nap, the spindle resting beside her. Later she was upright again, spinning away.

No boss was pushing her to do unsatisfying work just to eat and pay the bills. She had no bills. In fact, I never saw anyone exchange money while I was there. People worked when they wanted to work, rested when they wanted to rest, and shared whatever they produced.

Everywhere I looked, it was like a story too good to be true. Their kids were friendly and very capable. A little girl of 5 or 6 showed me how to spin cotton into yarn. She seemed like quite the expert. A boy of about 10 finished making an arrow as I watched, then invited me to target practice with his hand-made bow.

These self-sufficient people needed no police or prisons. Each member took responsibility for themselves and the good of the group. While I never saw any emotional outbursts or disputes, they were very willing to use violence to protect themselves if attacked. While walking between villages, I saw young men carry shotguns over their shoulders for protection from drug traffickers. Everyone was welcomed to protect themselves and each other as needed.

Even their leaders surprised me. When I arrived at one very far-away village, a small man greeted us with a warm smile and helped my friends and me settle in. I later learned he was the village leader, but he wasn't richer than average. When visiting his home, I noticed it was the same size and had the same items as everyone else's.

On Mike's suggestion, I made sure to bring a large sack of goods with me as gifts, including material for fishing, sewing, cooking, and anything else Mike had said they would find useful. I spent hundreds of dollars on it, and when they told me I could leave it in a home far from the village where I would be staying, I hesitated at first. Yet when I returned 2 weeks later with many Ashaninka to give out the gifts, I found the sack untouched, just as I had left it. This kind of widespread integrity was normal and unremarkable.

As I handed out the gifts, they seemed genuinely grateful, and no one asked for more. I felt happy to share but also sad that I didn't have more to give.

Given their integrity and generosity, I wasn't surprised that no one seemed concerned about robbery. I never saw a building with doors, much less locks. Few of their houses even had walls!

When it was time for me to go a week later, I did not want to say good-bye. All the Ashaninka I met seemed trustworthy, generous, capable, responsible, relaxed, joyful, and healthy – not just one or two individuals, but everyone I found. They had no courts, no police, no prisons, and no corrupt government. I did see people gathering in council on my last day as they discussed how to respond to Peruvians who were overfishing the nearby river.

Returning to the United States

I left the Ashaninka feeling both elated and confused.

A few months later, my father asked me what I had learned. I told him that I didn't know yet, and I was still figuring it out. But I knew this: people can live differently. We can treat each other well. I knew it was possible, and I would never doubt it again because I saw it with my own eyes.

The more I looked around in my own nation, the United States, the more urgent it seemed to figure out those lessons. Deceit, selfishness, ignorance, and unnecessary misery seem pervasive.

For example, the American legal system doesn't actually guarantee a fair trial like I learned growing up. It turns out that 98% of federal prisoners don't get a trial at all – prosecutors commonly threaten people with decades in prison, and then offer them a plea bargain. People are offered a shorter prison sentence if they admit their "guilt", regardless whether they're guilty or not. Afraid of losing at trial due to racism, inability to afford a lawyer, police deceit, or other reasons, many people accept this offer. So for 98% of prisoners, the legal system and public have no idea whether they're actually guilty![116]

I realized that driving past a prison is like driving past a chattel slave plantation from two centuries ago: the slaves didn't "deserve" to be there; they were just captured and enslaved and put to work, or else they'd get punished. How are present-day prisoners in a different situation, if only 2% got a trial by jury where they actually got a chance to defend themselves in court? Prisoners cannot legally refuse to work either, just like chattel slaves of the past. It's like an ancient injustice just changed form, but never really went away.

Everywhere I look in my town, I see the same kind of corruption, each industry in its own way.

I went grocery shopping, and found that almost everything for sale causes problems like cancer, immune disorders, and developmental disorders: from pesticides in the food, to plastic wrapping, to non-stick coatings on pans.[172,157,179]

Going to a pharmacy, I saw the same corruption there: drug after drug produced by pharmaceutical companies with a long track record of problems like fraud, misleading advertising, bribing government officials, and manipulating research trials.[13]

The Ashaninka don't have corruption like this. What lessons could I possibly learn from them to help make this nightmare end?

I drive past all the major banks every day – the same banks that keep getting "caught" every few years laundering money for drug cartels and human trafficking organizations, or forging legal paperwork to defraud homeowners, cheating their own customers, or whatever the next scam-of-the-day is.[288]

These pharmaceutical companies and banks get dinged with little "cost of doing business" fines by the government, and nothing much changes. The predatory and selfish behavior continues – not by outsiders, but mostly people within my own nation! How come the Ashaninka are able to maintain respectful relations between everyone, and in America, it seems like rich Americans are the biggest threat that the poor Americans face?

Almost all of America's drinking water is now toxic, with different regions having their own mix of heavy metals, microplastics, and other chemicals. Chemical and fossil fuel companies don't seem to care about the long term effects of the products they sell.[259]

Forests keep getting cleared to make way for strip malls and suburban lots, while scientists sound the alarm that loss of forests is a major driver of climate change and the mass extinction happening right now.[57]

Anyone who confronts injustices and tries to uphold the law is punished, because only the police are supposed to enforce the law. Unfortunately, the police have to follow orders and clearly they don't enforce the law consistently. As a result, no one is free to confront these terrible troubles.

I find disturbing stories at home too. My black roommate recently said that some white men had yelled at her to go back to her own country, wherever that was supposed to be. Another friend tells me stories of sexism anytime she describes her job.

These troubles put me in a pickle. I don't like being a downer, so when I'm with friends I usually try to keep it light and positive. That means we mostly have superficial conversations about our hobbies, jobs, or other things. If we talked about the most important issues like pollution, corporate greed, and dishonest politicians, there'd be plenty to discuss, but few people are willing to talk about that. After all, if we can't do anything about it, then what's the point of acknowledging all these things anyway?

What am I supposed to learn from the Ashaninka? How can they be humans like me and other Americans, and they live in such a beautiful way, while we don't?

Are the Ashaninka unique? Did they just get lucky, and Americans didn't? Are there societies like the Ashaninka, either now or in the recent past, where people treat each other and the Earth with respect, without discrimination, greed, and dishonest leaders? If so, could they help clarify the lessons that the Ashaninka have to offer?

It turns out, yes, there are more societies like the Ashaninka. Countless more!

What I've learned is nothing short of revolutionary for those of us not living this way now.

Part One of this book is about our human nature: *integrity, bravery, generosity, service, and intimate connection with the Earth – these are who we really are as humans*. Discrimination, hatred, greed, corruption, and exploitation are not part of human nature, they're not inevitable, and whole nations of people can live without them. They are symptoms of a disease, and just because a disease is common right now does not make it part of human nature.

Part Two explores *how we lost our way,* why some nations are stuck with these troubles generation after generation.

Part Three calls for *The Deepest Revolution:* our current way of life isn't working, so we must embrace an ancient way of life where respect is the norm. This will take tremendous integrity, generosity, and bravery, and it's worth it.

The Deepest Revolution draws stories and quotes from many sources, including many books written by people of healthy nations themselves such as Robin Kimmerer's *Braiding Sweetgrass* about the Potawatomi and Martín Prechtel's *Secrets of the Talking Jaguar* about the Tzutujil Maya. Other sources come from people who interviewed or spent extended time with people of healthy nations, such as Anne Cameron's *Daughters of Copper Woman* about the Nootka and Frank Linderman's *Pretty Shield* about the Crow. It also draws from my own research, much of which was published in *One Disease One Cure*.

While each healthy nation is unique, there are common aspects of their way of life that enable them to maintain a baseline of mutual respect, and this book aims to explore those common patterns based on the words of people from healthy nations or respectful observers.

The next chapter shows how the Ashaninka are not the exception. *They are the norm.* Those of us living in unhealthy nations that now dominate much of the Earth are *not* the norm.

Widespread racism, sexism, child abuse, pollution, corruption, crime, domestic violence, and all the rest may seem "just the way life is," but that's not true. The Ashaninka and many other healthy nations show us who we really are as humans. These troubles are not the result of supposedly-selfish human nature. If enough of us wake up and cultivate the courage, we can live without these troubles again.

Revolutionary Activity #1
Imagine a whole nation of caring people

Take 5 minutes to imagine your life if everywhere you went, people welcomed you, fed you, sheltered you, protected you and included you like family. Imagine also if they trusted that you would show the same care for them as a normal way of life. How does that feel?

Chapter 2: Can Whole Nations Embrace Generosity and Integrity?

My time with the Ashaninka felt shocking, but it turns out their generous and respectful way of life is not exceptional at all. There are many nations around the world, large and small, where people live or lived in traditional times with generosity and integrity towards each other for millions of years. Cooperation and mutual respect was – and in a few places, still is – the norm, not the exception.

What is not at all normal, in terms of our basic human nature, is how people live in the United States and every other unhealthy nation, past and present, that have dominated and warped people for millennia.

Because most people alive today have never experienced nation-wide generosity and respect, the corruption, greed and discrimination may seem inevitable, part of every human society.

But we can do much better.

No Police, No Prisons, No Widespread Crime

One striking difference between healthy nations living in traditional times compared to what we generally think of as 'normal' is their remarkable lack of prisons, police, and crime.

Can you even imagine living in a nation without crime?

I was amazed to discover that the Ashaninka have no police or prisons, yet they also seem so relaxed and unconcerned about crime. There are no locked doors. In fact, they don't have doors!

Avoiding crime may seem impossible in societies numbering in the thousands or more, yet many large healthy human nations have lived this way – not just occasionally, but for millions of years.

Many Americans and Europeans, when encountering healthy nations for the first time, have been surprised by the lack of crime or law enforcement. For example, when French Christian missionaries first visited the Huron in North America in the 1600s, they were amazed that thousands of people could get along so well without police or prisons.[279]

In the 1930s, when American dentist Weston Price visited many healthy nations around the world, he wrote, "few impressions can be more vivid than that of the absence of prisons and asylums."[225]

Benjamin Franklin seemed equally impressed by healthy nations he visited in the 1700s: "All their government is by Counsel of the Sages. There is no Force; there are no Prisons, no officers to compel Obedience, or inflict Punishment."[154]

Indeed, Haudenosaunee writers noted, "We have no jails and do not need them."[209]

In sharp contrast, the United States, France, and every other unhealthy nation around the world spend huge amounts of time, energy, and money trying to control crime with prisons and police – and yet so much crime and political corruption continues.

How can some nations live without police and prisons, and also no widespread crime, while other nations, chock full of police and prisons, have so much crime?

It's not as if healthy nations don't have some troubles – in any society, people sometimes don't get along. One difference is that they address disputes in ways that maintain a baseline of mutual respect among everybody, holding people to high standards of good behavior without demanding humiliation or submission. And when mutual respect is the norm, any selfish or hurtful act stands out as something to be immediately addressed so everyone can return to that respectful baseline.

Priscilla Settee, a woman of the Cree people, described their reconciliation process where elders would consider how to bring a person "back into a balanced life" and help them "focus on what is important in life." Instead of believing that a troubled person is bad and deserves punishment, this more loving approach recognizes that the troubled person is basically good but off-balanced or missing something important. The goal is to help them regain their balance.[184]

The Ju/'hoan San (these punctuation symbols refer to sounds that don't exist in English) have healing dances for people who aren't getting along, where they "put these two people next to each other so that they can come into harmony by dancing together… it's a technology of opening the heart so that healing energy can enter and so that people's hearts will be revealed to each other and any problems or enmity will go out from between them."[187]

So What's Their Secret?

How do healthy nations mostly avoid crime? Isn't selfish, violent, or otherwise bad behavior just an unfortunate part of human nature?

Actually, no. As later chapters show, when people live in respectful societies where everyone stands for what's right and gives generously as a normal way of life, the motivation to behave selfishly is greatly diminished.

And when trouble does arise, misbehaving people get counseled at first, and the response escalates if the misbehavior continues. This gives people a chance to course-correct without the extreme stress, danger, and humiliation of being imprisoned.

Traditional Potawatomi emphasized sharing and strongly discouraged selfishness. In Robin Kimmerer's book *Braiding Sweetgrass,* she explained how anyone who took too much, to the detriment of the community, was "first counseled, then ostracized, and if the greed continued, they were eventually banished…"[130]

Banishing or killing someone for severe misbehavior, like hoarding wealth or killing someone in anger, appears to have been very rare.

All these nations seem so different, each with their own ways of helping people get along, resolving disputes, and addressing anybody's selfish or hurtful behavior. But one way or another, people of healthy nations have or had ways of maintaining a baseline of mutual respect. That is, they found ways to maintain solidarity and respectful relations among everyone inside the nation as a normal way of life.

But Can We Live This Way Today?

Yes! There are present-day examples of people who struggled with greed, discrimination, and corruption for centuries, but then founded a new healthy nation and did away with these problems. The Zapatistas were conquered by the Spanish 500 years ago, then lived under Mexican rule until their revolution in 1994. Even after so long, they remembered how to have a healthy nation. When they launched their revolution, they knew how to re-establish that baseline of mutual respect among themselves even while under attack from the Mexican military.[233]

As just one example, the Zapatistas substantially reduced the sexism that women faced. When women were interviewed 20 years later in 2014, one said "The capitalists had us believing this idea… that women are not valuable." Another woman said, "The [women] suffered a lot before '94: humiliation, mistreatment, rape." But the revolution brought deep change, with one Zapatista woman saying "As women we have the same rights as men, we have the right to decide which duties we can carry out in the communities…" Another woman said, "in those [Mexican] organizations there are many problems of rape and mistreatment, while with us, Zapatistas, it is not that way…"[170]

The Zapatistas show that even people who have lived with sexism, greed, and corruption for centuries can still come together, create a healthy nation, and choose to live without these troubles.

Of course, there are many stories of individual Americans or small groups pulling together in times of crisis or generally acting with kindness toward others. But a whole nation? Or even a whole town? Besides the Ashaninka, I have never seen a whole nation or town of honest, giving, respectful people. Have you?

And yet as I read more about various healthy nations living in traditional times, I kept finding stories in which whole towns and even whole nations routinely acted with kindness and respect toward every member.

Nancy Basket, a woman of Cherokee descent, described how such kindness was maintained even as villages grew. When traditional Cherokee towns got larger than 600-700 people, hunting and foraging became difficult. Recognizing that the town needed to split into two, a new town site was agreed upon, often about seven miles away. They didn't have rich people and poor people, so that the poorest couldn't afford housing and had to leave or fend for themselves. Instead, everyone would go build the new homes and other structures regardless whether they were planning to live there or not. They even made sure all the gardens were planted.[25]

People would go back and forth between the new and old sites as they prepared the new town. Everyone took responsibility for their neighbors' wellbeing. Like people in all healthy nations in traditional times, they lived by the golden rule, each person treating the others the way they would want to be treated.

Trustworthy and Generous

I kept finding stories of nations that currently or in the recent past were similar to the Ashaninka. Superficially, of course, they were and are different – Eskimos in the arctic might have very different clothes, food, or ceremonies than the Gumbaynggirr of Australia, or the Jenu Kuruba in Asia. But I kept noticing deep, beautiful patterns that healthy nations seem to all share in common when they are able to live in a traditional way.

Besides the lack of police and prisons, I also noticed observers remarking on their deep integrity. When Ohiyesa, a Sioux man born in the 1800s, visited an American city, he said, "I was cautioned against trusting strangers, and told that I must look out for pickpockets. Evidently there were some disadvantages connected with this mighty civilization, for we Indians seldom found it necessary to guard our possessions."[64]

American S.M. Barrett described having complete trust in Apache leader Geronimo, saying, "When he once gives his word, nothing will turn him from fulfilling his promise."[20]

Stanley Vestal and George Grinnell also described how they found the Sioux and Cheyenne people completely trustworthy, sounding just like my experience with the Ashaninka.[286]

I remember first reading about Geronimo's integrity, and my mind went to all the untrustworthy politicians in the United States – and also every other country I'd visited, including Ecuador, Peru, Germany, Great Britain, and Canada. Some individuals in these countries are trustworthy, but none of these nations has anything like the universal integrity I'd experienced with the Ashaninka, or like these other observers in the 1800s experienced with the Sioux, Cheyenne, and many other beautiful nations.

And it's not just trustworthiness. I kept finding stories of incredible generosity – not just occasionally, but as a normal way of life for whole nations.

Jesuit Christian missionaries in the 1600s noted that the Huron would never let someone go without food or shelter. When someone's house burned down in the Huron village Ossossane, their neighbors came together to build a new one. Instead of having markets for trading or bartering, they embraced hospitality, gift-giving, and ceremonial exchanges. Visitors to a village were given food and shelter for as long as they wished to stay.[277]

The Huron would publicly announce whenever someone donated a large amount towards a feast, funeral, or ceremony, and this raised the donor's status. People thus enjoyed accumulating goods so that they could give away as much as possible, and thus earn their neighbors' gratitude. Feasts were common as people sought to build up their stash of food only to give it away.[277]

How amazing would it be to live in a society where people don't accumulate money to hoard it and enrich themselves, but gather wealth so they can share it with their neighbors?

This wasn't unique to the Huron, and these practices aren't just from the distant past. The Tzutujil Mayans were able to maintain their traditional way of life until about 1990, and Martín Prechtel described how they had a "self-impoverished theocracy" where people "loved to get more than someone else, just so they could dress fancily and give it all away to be big." Prechtel wrote how the Tzutujil Mayans became leaders: "To get anywhere in traditional Mayan society, you had to work really hard to get wealth, get appointed to office without campaigning, and then give it all away."

Each time a leader rose to a new level in their hierarchy, he or she gave away all their things so that they were equally as impoverished as everyone else.[221,220]

Haudenosaunee writers, in their book *Basic Call to Consciousness*, described similar generosity in their traditional leaders: "To become a political leader, a person is required to be a spiritual leader; and to become a spiritual leader, a person must be extraordinarily generous in terms of material goods."[201]

When Even Prisoners of War Don't Want to Leave

All this could easily seem too good to be true, except for another kind of story I kept finding: stories of people born in unhealthy nations running away to live in healthy nations.

Benjamin Franklin also noticed this, saying "No European who has tasted [Indian] Life can afterwards bear to live in our societies."[153] Many enslaved people who escaped European bondage also ran away to live with healthy nations.[154]

Even when people of unhealthy nations were captured in war, they commonly liked living in a respectful society so much that they wanted to stay. When the French and Haudenosaunee engaged in an exchange of war prisoners in 1699, Cadwallader Colden noted how the French didn't want to return home after experiencing life in a healthy nation: "…notwithstanding the French Commissioners took all the Pains possible to carry Home the French, that were Prisoners with the [Haudenosaunee], and they had full Liberty from the Indians, few of them could be persuaded to return."[282]

French prisoners of war had lived in a non-abusive society and liked it so much that few could be persuaded to go home. Colden noticed that this wasn't unique to the French, as "the English had as much Difficulty" and he wrote that this uneven prisoner exchange "has been found true on many other Occasions."[282]

This was obviously humiliating for colonial leaders who pretended not to abusively exploit their citizens, but it got worse. In a big prisoner exchange on the Muskingum River in 1764, white people had won out against the local healthy nations in war, but European leaders found the prisoner exchange unsatisfying. People of healthy nations who had been trapped in European prisons ran back to their communities with great joy. But when "civilized" Europeans got a little taste of living in a society where integrity, sharing, and reciprocity were a way of life, many desperately wanted to stay.[282]

In fact, many white captives had to be *dragged away with their hands and feet tied* to keep them from running back to the healthy nation they'd been able to experience.[282]

These healthy nations were a major threat to colonial leaders, because they showed that it was possible to live in a respectful way, without a few people ruling over the rest, without rich and poor, corruption, and all the injustices that unhealthy nations always experience. This explains why many European colonial leaders deliberately spread lies and hateful propaganda, such as calling people of healthy nations devil-worshippers and savages. Many colonial leaders in North America also punished anybody who tried to run away to live with nearby healthy nations.[153]

Deep Respect, Even when Capturing Prisoners of War

For a while I wondered how healthy nations could keep prisoners of war if they don't have prisons. I also had heard of some of these nations killing their captives – how does that square with being a culture based on generosity and integrity?

There are three ways to deal with war captives that allow a nation to maintain a baseline of mutual respect internally: release the captive, kill them, or integrate them and treat them well. Killing or releasing captives maintains that baseline of mutual respect among everyone within the nation, and even killing can be an act of service to one's neighbors if it helps protect the group. But once captives are accepted as residents, they are treated respectfully too.

People of healthy nations openly acknowledged that in traditional times they treated their captives with respect, as that baseline of mutual respect really does apply to anyone within the nation. Ohiyesa wrote, "It was a point of honor in the old days to treat a captive with kindness."[71]

Pretty Shield, a woman of the Crow nation, described how captive people were treated with the same decency as everyone else. When asked about captured women, she said, "because they were treated well they never tried to get away. They had the same rights as Crow women, and worked no harder." A Lakota woman named Goodtrader was captured by the Crows and ended up having a loving family and later refused to return to the Lakota when she had the chance.[148]

Healthy nations do not incorporate captives as a permanent underclass of servants, which would create exploitative relationships within the nation. Even in the difficult situations created by war, they keep that internal baseline of mutual respect.

These stories show that the Ashaninka's beauty isn't unique. Every nation is different, but there are common patterns that allow whole nations to maintain a baseline of mutual respect internally. People embrace integrity and generosity towards their neighbors, and have systems of conflict resolution that work while avoiding unaccountable police and punitive prisons. Because generosity was or is so common, they don't have rich and poor, and leaders serve everyone.

How do they do it? If a group of people wanted to live in such a beautiful way, what lessons could they learn from the Ashaninka and all these other healthy nations to make that possible?

Revolutionary Activity #2
Did you know?
Are you surprised to learn that healthy nations have existed for millions of years, including today, where people treat each other with generosity and respect? Did you think that such ways of living are unrealistic? Think of any assumptions you have about people that you may now question.

Chapter 3: Healthy Nations Share Three Core Spiritual Practices

I kept finding stories of nations that reminded me of the Ashaninka, such as the Yequana, Apache, Haudenosaunee, and Lakota. Due to centuries of violence from unhealthy nations, not all these nations can live in a traditional way today like the Ashaninka. While these nations have their differences, during traditional times they all live or lived in a similarly beautiful way.

Eventually I heard about a self-study program called Kamana (now called *Living Connection 1st*). The program promised to help people connect with the Earth using similar practices, stories, and attitudes as in many of the nations I was reading about. The lead author, Jon Young, had received mentorship and guidance from sub-chief Jake Swamp of the Mohawk nation within the Haudenosaunee Confederacy, Ingwe who was raised by the Akamba people in Kenya, Gilbert Walking Bull and Tony Ten Fingers of the Lakota, and Tom Brown Jr who received extensive training from Stalking Wolf, an Apache man.[299,298]

The Kamana program seemed like a synthesis of what Jon Young had learned from people of all these nations with the goal for the student to develop a deep, personal connection with the Earth.

Little did I know that Kamana would introduce me to spiritual practices which are common in all healthy nations. I believe that many of the other shared characteristics of healthy nations, past and present, flow from this spiritual foundation.

The First Core Spiritual Practice: A Practical, Aware Gratitude

I learned directly about the first spiritual practice of *cultivating a practical, aware gratitude* for the gifts of life by repeatedly immersing myself in the natural world. I went to the same place every day and observed the nonhumans. At first, I felt a bit bored. But the more I observed the world around me, the more I learned.

Over time, I learned which plants are edible, and which trees offer good wood for burning. I studied the language of birds, and what they could tell me about the rest of the forest.

The more I learned how every creature contributes to the web of life, the more grateful I felt. Some trees are especially good at holding the soil in place on the edge of a stream – holding the soil down is a gift they give. Birds' songs can alert me to nearby animals that I cannot see myself. Animals give the gifts of meat for food and hides for clothing. Streams give water for drinking. The sun gives us all warmth and light.

All these things are gifts. No one makes the trees offer their gifts of shade or firewood. I can plant an apple tree and tend it, but I cannot make it bear fruit – that is its gift.

At first I wondered – how is meat a gift? Don't humans have to take it, killing animals that would rather live? When a nation of people has a reciprocal relationship with other animals, the humans actually benefit them. For example, when humans intentionally enrich deer habitat, there are more deer because of humans' presence, even including hunting. When this reciprocity exists, humans give their gifts to the deer community, and deer give their gifts in return, helping sustain the humans that sustain them.

The first core spiritual practice is to notice all the gifts we receive and feel grateful for them. Every healthy nation has its own ways of expressing gratitude, but they all have *some* way.

The Haudenosaunee have their beautiful Thanksgiving Address, where they methodically name many kinds of life and give thanks for the gifts of each one.[297] Okanagan woman Jeannette Armstrong described how they love other species as brothers and sisters.[183] Potawatomi woman Robin Kimmerer described how humans are the "younger brothers of Creation" and our older nonhuman siblings can teach many gifts of wisdom.[127]

I grew up learning to give thanks to God by closing my eyes and ignoring my surroundings to focus on the prayer. I prayed by thinking thoughts in my head, directed to my idea of God. And I thanked my mental idea of God for all the good things in life.

Instead of closing my senses and thinking a prayer to my idea of God, I practiced keeping all my senses wide open and giving thanks to all the beings directly for their gifts. Instead of just having the feeling of gratitude or giving thanks vaguely, I practiced noticing the practical ways each being helped me or contributed to the web of life all around, such as by teaching me something, feeding me or other animals, or shading the soil so it would stay moist. Paying attention and noticing all the gifts I received was the path to cultivating *a practical, aware gratitude* for the gifts of life.

Once I started seeing nonhumans as teachers and feeling grateful for them, I started learning lessons too. I'll never forget my first clear lesson from a nonhuman, a hunting lesson from red-shouldered hawks. I was walking through a forest and observed a single hawk flying and screeching overhead. Red-shouldered hawks hunt small animals like mice and shrews, so they would be acutely aware of the predator flying above. I assumed the hawk wasn't interested in hunting, since otherwise, why make so much noise?

I looked up through the forest canopy just in time to notice a second, silent hawk flying to the first one. Once they were together, the loud hawk flew away screeching, and the silent hawk flew in the opposite direction. If I were a little mouse, I might feel relief at hearing the loud hawk fly away, and if I relaxed my guard I might not notice the silent hawk flying right over me! The hawks taught me a way to use deception while hunting. They also taught me to question my assumptions.

Hawks hunting

Revolutionary Activity #3
Gratitude for the nonhumans' gifts

Cultivating a practical, aware gratitude begins with noticing the gifts you receive. To start, go outside and find a nonhuman to observe closely, and ask what its gifts are.

For example, if you observed a tree, you would ask: how does the tree benefit all the life around it, including you? One way to find out is to ask "what would be different if the tree weren't there?" Does the tree provide nest sites for birds? Does it give you privacy or provide beautiful greenery? Does it hold the soil in place to prevent erosion? Notice all the gifts that you can, and practice feeling grateful for them.

The Second Core Spiritual Practice: Giving Your Sacred Gifts

Through my nature connection practices, I learned so many ways each creature contributes to the web of life, but I had never wondered what *my* unique contribution could be. No one had ever told me this, but each human also has sacred gifts to give, just like all the plants and other animals. It only makes sense, since humans are divine creatures like everything else in Creation.

Once again, every healthy nation I studied recognized this to be true. Tony Ten Fingers described a Lakota phrase, "mitakuye oyasin," loosely meaning "everything is my relative." His elders also taught him a deeper meaning: "I have a burning desire in my heart to know how I fit into the Creation which is one living being."[295]

Nancy Basket, a woman of Cherokee descent, said "Each lifetime you come with a medicine, a purpose that only you can get done. If you don't get it done, it won't get done. That's how important each person is. What is it that you love to do?"[25]

Just like everybody else, you have sacred gifts, a life purpose, a way you can make the world a better place – *and only you can do it!* All of Creation is simply divine creatures giving their sacred gifts. Thus the second core spiritual practice is to *cultivate and give your sacred gifts* too.

Cultivating and giving one's sacred gifts fully is how a person gives their deepest love. Training a person to give their sacred gifts trains them to give their deepest love in life, and to be their best self.

Some people have a special calling to enrich the soil, find food during lean times, or mentor children. Others are fighters who protect their people, mediators who resolve conflict, or historians who keep ancient stories alive. I learned that it's up to each of us to find our sacred gift or gifts and our own unique way of making the world a better place. The Haudenosaunee teach that it's each of our responsibility to help each other find their gifts, since sometimes a person can struggle to discover them on their own.[296]

"Cultivating your gifts" means to develop any necessary skills and wisdom. For example, if you're a healer or fighter, then train to be the best healer or fighter you can be in service of people you love.

Like the Thanksgiving Address and cultivating a practical, aware gratitude, I had a hard time with this practice too. I had never thought about my life purpose or what I deeply loved to do. Mostly I'd focused on building a safe and comfortable life, and I'd never thought about what I would do or give if I didn't feel constrained by needing a job. When I thought about it, I felt stressed and anxious.

I knew I had a passion for learning and teaching self-defense even though I hadn't practiced in years. While continuing with the nature connection training, I enrolled in jiu jitsu martial arts classes. I was suddenly walking a more meaningful path, and I felt better.

These two spiritual practices of gratitude and gift-giving are both beautiful. The third core spiritual practice ties them all together.

The Third Core Spiritual Practice: Living in Reciprocity

Healthy nations like the Ashaninka, Cherokee, and Potawatomi remain alive around the world, even if many are not able to fully live in their traditional ways. One day I noticed something interesting: they keep showing up in the news. Often when some environmental catastrophe occurs or a selfish corporation threatens to pollute the Earth, I notice people of healthy nations standing in solidarity with the land.

The Sioux led the Dakota Access Pipeline protests in 2016 in North America, seeking to protect the water from oil spills.[292] In 2010, the Indian government evicted many Jenu Kuruba people from their ancestral land, supposedly to protect local populations of endangered tigers. The Jenu Kuruba noted that the tiger population was so high where they lived precisely because they worship the tigers, as well as the other nonhumans. "To worship" means "to respect," so the Jenu Kuruba live in a way that respects the tigers and takes their needs into account.[25] The Jenu Kuruba demanded to be allowed to return and that the Indian government stop giving mining companies leases on their homeland.[54,113]

In Africa, the Mbuti likewise rejected a government so-called "conservation" effort that tried to force them off their land while companies came to dig for gold. One hunter named Mapenzi said, "We know how to protect our forest because nobody knows it the way we do. We know where the animals give birth, where they sleep and during which periods one must never kill them... The animals that the modern law wants to conserve are already under our customary protection. These are the laws our ancestors established."[87] The Gumbaynggirr in Australia and Sami in northern Europe work to prevent logging old-growth forests.[120,248]

In South America, the Yuracare and Tchimane protect their forests as the Bolivian government wants to allow illegal road development, monocrop farming, and deforestation.[254] In northern Asia, the Evenk and Nivkh work to stop destructive Russian oil and gas extraction activities.[242]

Everywhere I looked, I noticed healthy nations were standing in solidarity with the Earth, sometimes even putting their lives on the line to do so. Eventually I understood this as the third core spiritual practice: *living in reciprocity*. This means you have a responsibility to give back to all the beings who give so much to you. This is not merely a nice idea; it is a core practice for individuals and groups who take responsibility for their human and nonhuman neighbors.

Robin Kimmerer noted how cultures of gratitude must incorporate reciprocity too, saying, "Each person, human or no, is bound to every other in a reciprocal relationship. Just as all beings have a duty to me, I have a duty to them." If you receive meat from an animal, you are bound to support the animal's community. When you eat corn, you have a responsibility to care for the soil it grows in. When you receive a river's gift of clear water, you are responsible for protecting the river. Kimmerer noted that learning and practicing these responsibilities is "an integral part of a human's education."[125]

People of healthy nations do not just avoid polluting the Earth; they actively support the nonhuman communities where they live.

> **Revolutionary Activity #4**
> **Give from gratitude**
> Do something kind and no-strings-attached for someone who has done something kind for you, or for anybody who looks like they need help. Get creative with what you can offer, such as helping move heavy things, lifting someone's spirits when they're feeling down, or helping them find a job. Practice feeling gratitude for what they've given you, or if they're a stranger, practice feeling thankful for what other strangers have given you, and give from that place of gratitude. Do not give in exchange or to "pay them back" because this is not a trade. Savor the pleasure of giving just for the joy of it.

Carry Your Gifts with Conviction

I believe that a person's spirituality is simply how they relate to themselves and the world. Is there an authoritarian god-figure scaring everyone into obedience? Is the world just a bunch of molecules moving around aimlessly? Or are we all divine beings, and it really matters how each of us shows up in life? The three core spiritual practices are spiritual because they teach people how to relate to the world: with practical, aware gratitude, by giving their deepest love, and living in reciprocity.

These three core spiritual practices are essential. You are the giving of your deepest love. Giving to others in gratitude for what we receive is who we are as humans.

People may learn to "hold back" or "shut down" parts of themselves to survive in their unhealthy nation, giving less than their deepest love. But anyone and any group can commit to embracing these practices. This book will explore how they encourage beautiful traits, including deep awareness, generosity, bravery, integrity, joy, and strong servant-leadership. And my more in-depth book, *One Disease One Cure,* explores these connections even further.

Is it any wonder that nations which embrace these spiritual practices are able to maintain respectful relations among their people, and between people and the Earth?

Anybody could embrace these practices right now to cultivate and give a deeper love. And what's good for the individual is also good for the group. As Kimmerer wrote, "in order for the whole to flourish, each of us has to be strong in who we are and carry our gifts with conviction, so they can be shared with others."[129]

What are your gifts? What can you give or do or be that would open your heart and let it sing?

Revolutionary Activity #5
Discover your own sacred gifts

You have sacred gifts to share, and there are many ways to find them. Choose one or more of these to help you identify your gifts: 1) Take time alone without distraction and feel in your heart what most matters to you, and how you can act in service of it. 2) Ask yourself what would be the most meaningful life you could imagine. 3) Notice what brings you special joy and or sparks curiosity. 4) Ask your friends when they have noticed you being the most joyful and engaged in life. 5) Notice what you feel angry about. Your anger can show you what you care about, or an injustice you want to make right.

If you do not get a clear answer quickly, have patience and keep investigating over time.

Chapter 4: Imagine If Generosity Was Normal

Picture living in a world where people routinely look out for each other's health and safety. A nation of neighbors who ensure each person has food to eat, tools to share, and a place to sleep. Imagine feeling deeply safe at every stage of life knowing that, even in times of scarcity, or war, you won't need to fend for yourself, because you live in a world where people take care of each other.

Is that hard to imagine?

In the United States, like every unhealthy nation, people generally do have to fend for themselves. Businesses must make a profit (take in more than they give out) or else they go under. And most people want to make as much money as possible too.

This drive to get more than we give (trying to "get" rich or trying to "get" ahead) is not our human nature. We are born naturally wanting to give and receive. However, an unnatural imbalance occurs in unhealthy nations, where the economy rewards selfishness and people who don't make enough money must live with sickness, hunger, homelessness, isolation, shame, and worse.

When you live in a nation where few people care if you have food to eat or a place to stay, the self-centered desire to take as much as possible (i.e. to get rich) is naturally pervasive, and as a result, it seems quite normal.

But is it?

Every healthy nation I've studied strongly promotes generosity (giving) and reciprocity (sharing with others who share with me over time) as a normal way of life. The following stories show what life is like when, instead of selfishness, generosity and reciprocity are normal.

Generosity from Birth

Traditionally, Sioux parents gave many feasts to celebrate their children's developmental milestones, including their first step, first spoken word, and first game killed. At each feast the parents gave away as much as they could for the benefit of those who had little.[70]

Sioux parents didn't just model generosity; they actively encouraged generosity in children from an early age. In one story, Red Cloud's community was going through a very hungry winter when his father finally hunted two elk. Red Cloud, at 4 or 5 years old, went and invited all the old people to come get food – without his parents' permission! His mother gave away almost all their food, and when young Red Cloud said he was hungry the next day, his mother did not admonish him. Instead she encouraged him to *be brave as he faced the consequences of his generosity*. She said, "Remember, my son, they went home singing praises in your name, not my name or your father's. You must be brave. You must live up to your reputation."[70]

Generosity Towards All Life

This generosity doesn't just exist between the people in these societies. In every single beautiful nation I found, their generosity extends to the nonhumans as well. That is, the people live or lived in a way that benefits the nonhumans around them.

Jeannette Armstrong described the traditional Okanagan decision-making process called en'owkinwiwx, and how it very carefully took into account the full range of the humans' and nonhumans' needs. She was trained as a *land speaker,* and her role in their group decision-making was to consider every decision's effects on the land. In this way, the Okanagans made sure to always take the nonhumans' needs into account.[183]

In his book *Wolf Totem,* Jiang Rong describes living with Mongolian hunter-shepherds. These people recognized that while wolves sometimes ate the people's sheep, the wolves also ate gazelles which would overeat and destroy the grassland if the wolves didn't keep them in check. Without the grassland, the sheep would die, and humans couldn't survive either. Thus the hunter-shepherds were very careful not to overhunt the wolves, ensuring the whole ecosystem could thrive.[240]

Generosity is the Norm

These stories really touched me, even shocked me. But in time I realized this way of life is simply normal in any healthy society where everybody encourages generosity and strongly discourages selfishness. When everybody in a nation bases their lives on the three core spiritual practices of gratitude, gift-giving, and reciprocity, generosity naturally becomes pervasive, including their generous leaders. They aren't necessarily generous to outsiders – often they have been, and sometimes they haven't. But within the nation, they maintain generosity as a normal way of life.

Growing up in a Christian family, I learned about Jesus Christ's extreme generosity as he gave away all his possessions and encouraged his followers to do the same. Now I know that his generosity only seemed "extreme" because I live in an unhealthy nation that normalizes greed, just like Rome in Jesus's time. Jesus Christ's generosity would just seem normal in healthy nations.[63]

Nancy Basket described one way that Cherokee women traditionally redistributed goods. In one ceremony, all the ladies would honor the oldest woman in town by bringing her gifts. They knew she didn't need all the stuff, but they trusted that she would know where the goods needed to go. This old woman would then distribute the gifts to whomever needed them the most. This is one way that the Cherokee moved things from the people who had them to the people who most needed them.[25]

Jesuit missionaries stayed with the Montagnais-Naskapi and noticed that men left household affairs almost entirely up to the women. Regardless how much food they brought in, it never lasted long because the women commonly shared the food with everyone. Paul Le Jeune wrote, "I have never seen my host ask a giddy young woman that he had with him what became of the provisions, although they were disappearing very fast." Generous sharing was simply normal.[10]

I've studied many different kinds of economies, including socialism in the Soviet Union, capitalism in the United States, or communism in China. They may seem very different, but at their core, all these economies encourage and require selfishness.

How do healthy nations of all kinds avoid hurtful selfishness?

Deliberately Avoiding Selfishness at All Costs

In every healthy nation I've found, people recognize that selfishness would be a tremendous threat if it were ever allowed to take hold, and they go to great lengths to help everyone feel comfortable with sharing generously.

Even in these nations, someone may occasionally not get along with others, or start to feel disconnected or distrustful. As a result, they may start acting selfishly, prioritizing their own needs over the needs of the group.

Robin Kimmerer described how the traditional Potawatomi responded when they noticed someone behaving selfishly. If someone refused to share, they first counseled the person to help them feel comfortable sharing again. If the person insisted on acting greedily, they then escalated to ostracizing and, if necessary, even banishing them.[130]

Kimmerer wrote, "It is a terrible punishment to be banished from the web of reciprocity, with no one to share with you and no one for you to care for." They set a strong energetic boundary, not allowing selfishness to take hold in their nation. After all, if some individuals began acting selfishly, others might feel the need to act selfishly to protect themselves, and soon selfishness might become pervasive in the society. And who would want to live in a nation with pervasive selfishness and greed?[130]

The traditional Haudenosaunee were likewise very aware of how terrible life would be if selfishness were allowed to take hold in their nation. They rejected systems of private property, and some Haudenosaunee wrote, "That idea (property) would produce slavery." They knew what kind of leaders would be chosen in any society that embraced private property and selfishness: "The acceptance of the idea of property would produce leaders whose functions would favor excluding people from access to property, and they would cease to perform their functions as leaders of our societies and distributors of goods."[202]

In other words, it's no accident that they maintain a way of life based on generosity and mutual respect. In every healthy nation I've found, they recognize the profound threat that selfish behavior represents, and they go to great lengths to avoid it.

Jeannette Armstrong's description of Okanagan decision-making shows how beautiful life can be in nations that embrace generosity and reciprocity, and why people would go to such great lengths to avoid selfishness. When a community includes the perspectives of human relationships and the land in their decision-making, "community changes... the material things don't have a lot of meaning... material wealth and the securing of it or being fearful and being frightened about not having 'things' to sustain you, disappears... The realization that people and community are there to sustain you creates the most secure feeling in the world... When that happens, you're imbued with the hope that others surrounding you in your community can provide."[183]

What Do These Stories Mean?

I started life bright and hopeful, thinking that things in the United States weren't so bad, and troubles with corruption, crime and pollution could be fixed. But I kept reading about endless corruption and didn't see a way out. Every political party seemed to be more part of the problem than part of a solution. Politicians kept getting corrupted after they were elected, and incorruptible politicians were killed or driven out. And the more I studied, the more I realized it had been this way throughout America's history.

I just kept seeing the same patterns of greed, discrimination, and corruption in every unhealthy nation, from Peru to North Korea to Russia, similar to the USA.

Over time I got jaded. It seemed like corruption is just part of human nature, an inescapable aspect of every nation. But these stories show that it really is possible to live in a beautiful way with other people, not just in a family or friendly neighborhood, but *we can have a whole nation where respect is the norm.*

For most of my life, I just did not know what a healthy nation looked like. I'd never found any "experts" who had any idea either.

Anybody can see political problems and have opinions about what to do, but without knowing what healthy nations are like, it's just speculation.

It's like if doctors only studied sick people but never encountered healthy people, and had no idea what "healthy" even looked like. Each doctor would have their own opinion, but without studying healthy people, their cures might not be helpful.

This is essentially what happens when most people debate political and cultural problems in their country. People who have never even heard of healthy nations, much less experienced one, try to diagnose social and political problems without knowing what a healthy nation is even like. People argue endlessly, and the political troubles just continue.

But we don't need to speculate about how to deal with our biggest political problems. Stories of healthy nations offer a *standard of comparison:* after studying common ways of life in these societies, such as how they avoid selfishness and encourage integrity and generosity, I could see the deep troubles in my unhealthy nation more clearly. Even better, these stories show a real path to creating whole nations where respect is just normal.

But first, we must answer a big question: why doesn't everybody live in healthy nations now?

Revolutionary Activity #6
Join or create a sharing group
We each have the ability to make generosity normal all around us. One way is to invite your friends together to found a *sharing group*. Find a way for the group to serve each of the individuals. For example, each month the group may travel to one person's home and help with home maintenance and gardening. Often the recipient will cook a big meal for everyone to celebrate after a long day. Another example: create a fund to which each person contributes $100/month, which your group can give or lend to anybody who needs help. Get creative and have fun thinking of how your sharing group can serve each other or a meaningful cause. Ensure each person has a way to contribute, and each person's contribution is recognized.

Chapter 5: Why Don't We All Live in Healthy Nations?

For years, I studied beautiful nations like the Lakota and Nootka living in traditional times, and I wondered what they have or had in common. They seem to avoid crime without police or prisons. Integrity and generosity are normal, and they have trustworthy leaders. People commonly respect each other and the Earth.

I also studied unhealthy nations like Russia, Great Britain, Canada, and the United States, and they have common patterns too, such as greed, selfish political leaders, and pollution. What causes those nations to be so unhealthy, generation after generation?

Do nations become unhealthy when the population gets too large? Some academic literature states that humans can only maintain tight knit communities of up to 150 people, a limit called "Dunbar's number." I commonly hear people claim that humans start behaving inappropriately towards each other in groups larger than 150, as accountability mechanisms supposedly start to break down then.[62]

But that doesn't make sense. The Ashaninka number more than 2,000 and people treat each other respectfully.

In 1674 CE, the Cherokee numbered about 50,000 and mutual respect was normal in their nation too.[159]

Do nations become unhealthy when they cover too much area? That doesn't make sense either. In the early 1700s, the Haudenosaunee Confederacy covered over 38,000 square miles.[102] This is similar to Switzerland, Bhutan, or Taiwan. If the Haudenosaunee were a US state, it would be the 38th largest, between Kentucky and Indiana.

Before extended European contact, the Cherokee covered about 40,000 sq miles. Clearly humans can maintain healthy nations that cover huge distances and include many thousands of people.[159]

Did the trouble happen when people started farming? No, the Huron gained about 75% of the food they ate from farming. They still shocked French missionaries who couldn't understand how people could get along without police, prisons, and authorities imposing law and order.[276,279] Even before the Europeans' arrival, the Haudenosaunee relied more on farming than hunting for food.[115]

Sometimes people of these nations are called native, indigenous, tribal, aboriginal, indian, or first nations. I call them healthy nations.

And they share one core difference from all unhealthy nations:

In healthy nations, everyone stands for a culture of mutual respect, and nobody rules over anybody else.

A nation is any group of people that protect each other from external threats and have their own laws, or their own standards of acceptable behavior that they hold each other to. In healthy nations able to maintain their traditional ways, everyone agrees on their laws, whereas in unhealthy nations, a few people decide on the laws and the rest are expected to obey them.

Furthermore, in healthy nations, people expect each other to *uphold* their law and seek justice. In unhealthy nations, people are expected to *obey* the laws they're given and they're punished for disobedience. They're also punished for upholding the law themselves and seeking justice directly. After all, enforcing the law is the police's job, though the police have to follow orders too.

In healthy nations, everyone stands for a culture of mutual respect, so they have strong leaders and nobody imposes law on anybody else. Everyone agrees on their rules for appropriate behavior, so they can live in a respectful way with each other and the Earth. And when someone behaves inappropriately, anyone may take initiative to ensure there is accountability. Such healthy nations may fight with each other, but within the nation, mutual respect is normal.

In unhealthy nations, one person or a few people rule over everyone else and demand obedience. Whether the rulers are kings, billionaires, imams, priests, prime ministers, or presidents, they impose laws that everyone else must follow or face severe punishment. The rulers choose how to enforce the law, and forbid the rest from directly holding misbehaving people accountable.

Rulers use all manner of tricks, traps, and childhood training to create and maintain obedience. In fact, racism, sexism, dishonest leadership, pollution, disconnection from nature, selfishness, widespread child abuse, and needless poverty are all merely *common symptoms caused by the root cultural disease* where some people rule over everyone else, and people accept their own submissive obedience as legitimate and normal.

Every nation where a person or group imposes law on the rest has the same kinds of troubles. For example, racism might "look" different in one unhealthy nation compared to another. But they all have some kind of racism, with groups of higher and lower privilege. These troubles do not exist in societies where everyone stands for what's right, confronting injustice as needed.

That is very good news! It means there is a way to live without so many problems like discrimination, greed, and pollution. The path to ending these problems is also the path to freedom. We must work together to create new nations where everyone agrees on their laws and everyone bravely upholds them as a normal way of life, taking humans' and nonhumans' needs into account.

In order to find a pathway to freedom and live without these terrible troubles, we must first be clear on what "freedom" even means.

Spiritual Strength and Freedom

Spiritual strength is foundational for maintaining a free, healthy nation. But what do "freedom" and "spiritual strength" even mean?

To me, a person has *spiritual strength* if they give their deepest love in each moment without holding back, and they stand for what's right for themselves and others.

Spiritual strength exists when you're clear on your sacred gifts and you give them each moment. In other words, you know what matters to you and you act in service of it. You do your best, even if you feel scared or uncertain in difficult moments.

Freedom exists when your neighbors *expect* you to stand for what's right and uphold the laws you live by, and you expect the same from them so that justice becomes normal. *In a free society, everyone is expected to stand for what's right, and no one is punished for it.* Everyone is expected to cultivate the spiritual strength needed for this way of life.

Standing for what's right means to carry out the golden rule, meaning to *treat others the way you would want to be treated.* If someone is attacked, protect them as you would want someone to protect you. If someone is hungry, share with them like you would want someone to share with you. In a free society, everyone expects themselves and everyone else to live by the golden rule.

However, if you live in a society with a ruling class, the police are the only ones allowed to enforce the law (and they have to follow orders). This means your unhealthy nation punishes you for seeking justice, even while abuses and corruption happen all around you. In unhealthy nations, no one is allowed to confront the deepest injustices. It is illegal to fully embrace the golden rule.

To survive in unfree nations, people learn to "hold back" or "shut down" parts of themselves and not even notice it just to get by, developing all sorts of emotional or spiritual wounds as explored in Part 2. These troubles represent a loss of that spiritual strength.

However, you can still stand for what's right and give your deepest love no matter what, even if you're trapped in an unhealthy nation that doesn't always welcome it. In other words, *you can have spiritual strength even if you don't have freedom.*

This clarifies why *freedom is built on spiritual strength:* when everyone in a nation gives their love and seeks justice in solidarity with others, then each person welcomes everyone else to do that too. When spiritual strength is normal in a nation, everybody stands in solidarity together so nobody experiences injustice.

When too many people "hold back" or "shut down" parts of themselves and learn to tolerate abuses all around, then we wind up with societies that punish people for standing for justice. Everyone in a nation must have that *spiritual strength* to give their deepest love and stand for what's right so that collectively they can have *freedom* where justice and mutual respect are normal.

Let's Be Brave Together

Later in this book, Part 3 explores how you can work with others to create a beautiful way of life, a new nation of spiritually strong people living in actual freedom. It offers ways to create deep relationships and healthy communities which will be the building blocks of new healthy nations based on the stories of others who have done this. This requires tremendous hard work, bravery and risk – and *it's worth it*.

But to understand why it's worth the risk, we must confront how deeply sick all unhealthy nations are, including yours. Recognizing the deep sickness will motivate you to build a way of life similar to how millions of people have lived since the dawn of time.

Anytime a ruling class takes hold, selfishness and exploitation become widespread and normalized. And since "selfishness" and "corruption" are the same, corruption becomes normal too.

The truth is that *your unhealthy nation is a trap* that keeps you and the people around you stuck in an unsatisfying way of life, generation after generation. In order to escape the trap, we must confront the deepest patterns of manipulation that have kept people trapped in unfree societies for centuries or millennia, even in so-called "democracies." Only with this deep understanding can we free ourselves and build truly healthy, free nations.

Many people avoid watching the news or thinking too deeply because "why bother" if you can't do anything about it? But what if you *can* do something? Most people just haven't heard the perspectives and stories that offer a helpful path.

The perspectives in Part 2 may feel hard to face alone. So let's be brave together and face the truth of unhealthy nations so we can see clearly why our current way of life isn't working, and why it never has. Together, we can uncover aspects of our own spiritual strength, and discover how people can build up each other's spiritual strength on the path to creating new beautiful nations.

To face the deep sickness in every unhealthy nation and learn ways to build spiritual strength, join me in *Part 2 - Why Are We So Lost?*

Part 2

Why Are We So Lost?

Chapter 6: Why Are We So Lost?

Everybody is born with a sense of dignity, meaning that we each have a *natural impulse to stand up for what's right* for ourselves and our neighbors. When people only live by laws they support, that urge to stand for what's right is also the urge to uphold the laws of their society and seek justice.

People of healthy nations have a common response when someone behaves disrespectfully towards their neighbors: they come together, discuss the problem, and consider how to respond collectively so they can return to that baseline of mutual respect that all humans expect from birth.

People born and raised in healthy nations during traditional times would be shocked if there were rich people, or if their leaders started giving money or special treatment to the rich while others went hungry or lived a precarious life. Or if rich businessmen used violent thugs to suppress people's efforts to get safe working conditions. Or if police arrested someone for saying the truth. Or if a loved one was falsely convicted of a crime, and the racist or sexist judge showed no interest in real justice.

And they would be shocked if they were threatened with severe violence for trying to end these injustices.

But for many of us living in the United States, Spain, Russia, China, Egypt, and every other unhealthy nation around the world, this is not so shocking, is it?

Why does such unjust behavior persist?

Fierce Resistance to Justice

Countless groups of people have tried countless times over centuries to come together and seek justice in their unhealthy nation. And when they do, what do they face, time and time again?

Regardless of the particular country, or the type of government or economy, whenever and wherever people in unhealthy nations seek justice, they face a similar response.

In socialist Venezuela, when students came together to seek better conditions at their university during an economic crisis in 2018, they saw this:[2,52]

Riot Police in Venezuela

In communist China, when people came together to stop corporations from polluting their rivers in 2012, they saw this:[104]

Riot Police in China

And in the capitalist United States, when protesters confronted illegal police violence towards black people in 2020, they saw this:[249]

Riot Police in the United States

I was taught growing up that the police's job is to keep people safe and enforce the law. But the riot police consistently protect the interests and possessions of the rich and powerful even when they are clearly violating the law.

And who are the police protecting the rich and powerful from? Of course, they protect the rich and powerful from people who are angry about low wages, pollution, corruption, wars based on lies, and all the usual injustices in unhealthy nations.

Anyone who obediently follows orders gives up their responsibility to serve their people and becomes the servant of whoever gives the orders. Corrupt leaders thus use obedient police to scare people away from standing up for themselves and seeking justice.

This is what it means to live in an unfree, unhealthy nation: people are threatened and punished for seeking justice.

In unhealthy nations, where people are forbidden from holding their leaders accountable or standing with others to seek justice, is it any wonder that so many leaders indulge in corruption and crime?

To anyone born in an unhealthy nation, this may seem natural. But healthy nations living in traditional times do not live this way.

Every single human feels a deep urge to stand up for what's right, though many have learned to ignore it. *Your urge to "stand for what's right" is your natural desire to uphold the laws of your own nation and seek justice.* In healthy nations, people are expected to act on that urge because they only live with laws that they actually support. In unhealthy nations, people are trained to repress that urge and are punished for acting on it. In addition, many people are forced to live with laws they don't support – another sign of living in an unfree society.

Unhealthy nations systematically train people from childhood to "hold back" or "shut down" parts of themselves so they won't honor this urge to confront abusive authorities and seek justice. Each person responds in their own way. People can learn to habitually ignore certain feelings or urges, develop narrow-minded, selfish or hurtful attitudes, or ignore some aspects of reality, leading to all kinds of strange emotional and spiritual disturbances.

In healthy nations, standing for what's right in solidarity with neighbors is not just allowed – it's expected. Everyone agrees on their laws, and everyone is expected to uphold them to ensure they can maintain a respectful way of life. Children are trained to have the spiritual strength to consistently confront any injustice.

This shows why so many people of unhealthy nations are lost, with ineffective politics and endless corruption, greed, discrimination, and pollution, no matter who people vote for. When the path to universal justice is outlawed – because people are forbidden from taking responsibility to choose and uphold their own laws – *injustice and ineffective political movements become normalized.*

As long as people accept their own submissive obedience as legitimate, they will be distracted by endless political debates that ignore the root problem. People may debate political issues looking at left-wing vs right-wing, republican vs democrat, capitalism vs communism, or monarchy vs democracy, but all these are tyrannical as long as a few people impose the law, and the rest obey it. Only when people stop accepting their own submissive obedience as legitimate can they begin to have meaningful political conversations.

Can you imagine living in a society where everyone accepts responsibility for seeking justice and upholding their laws, with everyone acting in solidarity to ensure that no one is mistreated? Few people have heard stories of how a whole village or nation can stand in solidarity, not just as an abstract idea but as a practical way of life. Let's look at an example so you can see what it's like.

> **Revolutionary Activity #7**
> **Stand for what's right**
> When you act on your urge to stand for what's right, you bring justice, connection, and understanding into the world. Think about a time you saw someone disrespected, misunderstood, cheated, or attacked, whether on TV or in person. How did you respond? How could you have taken a stand to make the situation turn out better? Look for another instance where someone around you is disrespected, and find a way to help address the disrespect so it doesn't happen again.

The Nootka Stand in Solidarity

In healthy nations that maintain their traditional ways, everyone upholds their laws as a normal way of life, protecting each other whenever the need arises. One story from the Nootka illustrates what life is like when everyone stands in solidarity to ensure that no one is disrespected.

In the book *Daughters of Copper Woman,* a Nootka storyteller described a cultural technique the Nootka used to help people see their own foolish behavior: people who acted like mirrors, helping other people see their own silly or foolish behavior by imitating it.[35]

These "mirror" people were like magazine opinion writers who commented on all sorts of things. If a mirror thought that the council was about to do something foolish, they might show up at council and imitate one of the leader's every moves so that "every little wart on that person would show, every hole in their idea would suddenly look real big."[35]

If a person were vain about their clothes, a mirror might follow behind them wearing tattered rags and their hair would be like a bird's nest full of mud and sticks, all looking similar to the vain person. If a person had a bad temper, a mirror might follow and have fits, hitting the sand with a rock or insulting birds and generally looking foolish. If a person became self-important, the mirror might follow along babbling like a baby, "until you finally heard what an ass you were bein'." And if a mirror started being mean or pushy, a second mirror might follow along and let the first one see how they were showing up.[35]

The Nootka storyteller noted, "nobody would ever dare blow up at the [mirror]!" Anyone who did would be confronted. Mirrors did not make fun of people or act hurtfully. They helped people see what they looked like to others and how ridiculous it was to put so much emphasis on unimportant things like clothes or jewelry, "instead of what counts, like bein' nice to people, and bein' lovin'..."[35]

Christians arrived and started dividing up the land. They set up a church, and began trying to get the Nootka to attend, offering glass mirrors and other trinkets as enticements. At church, the preacher told them what to wear, how to live, and what to do. He insisted that men shouldn't wear kilts, and women should only have long dresses that covered them completely. He kept saying that everyone should live and dress like the white man.[35]

One day, a mirror woman from a nearby community arrived at the church. Like the white man, she wore a big black hat and a black jacket. She even wore old rundown shoes someone had thrown away. Unlike the white man, she wore nothing else.[35]

She moved to the front and waited for church to start.[35]

The preacher got very upset, but everyone else looked at her respectfully. No one mocked her or looked away to avoid her nakedness.[35]

The preacher started ranting about nudity, naked women, sin, and respect for God. Then he came down from his pulpit and grabbed the mirror to throw her out![35]

Acting violently towards a mirror was absolutely not allowed, and the storyteller said, "The people just about ripped him apart." But the mirror protected him from the crowd, went up to where the preacher had been, and began speaking.[35]

The mirror first encouraged empathy, asking people to imagine how a stranger might feel, being away from home and surrounded by others who looked and acted differently. Then she reminded her neighbors that "there was more than one kind of mirror. There was the white man's mirror that you got if you went to church, but there was the mirror in the eyes of the people you loved…" She warned the crowd against following anybody like the preacher "who was so mixed up they'd do forbidden things."[35]

I feel impressed that this woman calmly and clearly confronted the preacher's hurtful attitudes. She even invited her neighbors to have compassion for a stranger after he'd acted rudely. I also feel impressed that the people immediately recognized who was in the right and acted in support of the mostly-naked woman instead of the self-righteous man. This story shows that whole communities can act in solidarity and stand for a culture of mutual respect when conflict arises.

This story also shows what it's like when everyone in a nation upholds the rules for how people treat each other. The Nootka didn't have police; everybody took a stand to protect the mirror when she was attacked. They had rules that worked for everyone, and everyone had the spiritual strength to uphold them.

And this solidarity was not a one-off event. It was a way of life. The mirror walked out of the church, and all the people followed her, leaving the preacher alone. That church still exists and remains empty to this day.[35]

Revolutionary Activity #8
Support someone else when they take a stand

The mirror-woman showed integrity by standing for the values that she wanted in her nation. Consider: how much harder would it have been for her to take that stand if she didn't trust others to stand with her? In other words, how much easier was it for her to take a stand knowing that others would support her?

Think of a time when you wanted to take a stand in some way – perhaps because a bully was picking on someone, or a boss made a rude remark in public, or a teacher was rude to a student, or a company was polluting the Earth. Were you scared to speak up and confront them because you worried you'd be alone? How amazing would it feel knowing you could take a stand and you could trust others to support you?

Just like you would want others' support in difficult moments, they want yours too. Your support makes it easier for other people to act with integrity. Look for an opportunity to support someone else who "sticks their neck out" to do the right thing, even when it's unpopular.

Solidarity and Generosity Used to be Universal

A few thousand years ago, every human on Earth lived in a healthy nation where solidarity and widespread generosity among neighbors was normal and expected.

In recent times, unhealthy nations have formed and spread around the world, trapping free people in abusive societies where a few people rule over the rest.

Why are we so lost then? The problem is simple – *we're not free, but we pretend that we are*. We don't choose the laws we live by; authorities impose laws and punish us for disobeying them. We're not allowed to stand for justice and uphold our own laws, because law enforcement is the police's job, and they have to follow orders.

We're not free, and any political movement that doesn't address this root problem is destined to achieve superficial change at best.

When standing in solidarity to seek justice is outlawed, fear and insecurity become widespread and put people in an isolated survival mode that breeds and rewards selfishness and disrespect. Instead of pervasive generosity, selfishness is pervasive at every level in every unhealthy nation.

When a generation of people cannot free themselves, that fear, insecurity, and selfishness can start to sink in and seem "just how life is." People can likewise raise their children to absorb fear, insecurity, and selfishness so they seem normal. But they're not normal.

You may not feel this affects you. Maybe you have enough goodies in your life or your race is privileged enough that you think you have escaped it. But ask yourself this: if you woke up tomorrow morning with no money, no food, no shelter, no credit cards or cell phone, and no one to call to help you out, what would your unhealthy nation do for you? Would you have the deep security that comes from living in a loving, healthy nation where nobody would let you starve or be treated disrespectfully? Would you have the deep security that comes from living among others who would stand with you against injustice?

Regardless of which unhealthy nation you live in, and no matter how "safe" you feel, the answer is no. And because you know that, you have known since childhood that you must play along.

But "playing along" is not who we really are. And that means each of us – including you – has the power to help make things right.

For many of us, we and our ancestors have been trapped in this way of life for a very long time. This may be painful to face, but we absolutely can – and we must – face the truth and stand up together to change it.

Revolutionary Activity #9
Notice when you hold back out of fear

Everyone has an urge to stand for what's right, but many learn to hold back out of fear, such as fear of losing friends, angering a spouse, or losing a job. To cultivate spiritual strength, notice when you feel afraid and hold back.

Recall a time when you felt an urge to do a good deed, speak out, or stand up for someone else, but you held back. What were you afraid of? Next time you feel afraid, notice the fear and find the bravery to do what you need to do.

Chapter 7: Why Are People So Selfish?

In every healthy nation I've studied, elders train children to be generous and to see selfishness as a threat to their way of life.

Sioux man Sitting Bull said, "Love of possessions is a disease,"[71] and Sioux man Ohiyesa described how he "was trained to be a warrior and a hunter, and not to care for money or possessions, but to be in the broadest sense a public servant."[66] Potawatomi woman Robin Kimmerer described how traditional elders would tell children scary stories of what might happen if they act selfishly.[130]

When one or a few people act selfishly, the nation can respond by helping them feel comfortable sharing again, or if necessary, evict them if they continue to behave selfishly.

But what happens when a ruling class forces laws on the rest, protecting their own wealth at all costs and forbidding people from standing for what's right? What happens when selfishness is systematically rewarded and maintained, and people can no longer maintain a way of life based on sharing?

Profit Economies Reward and Maintain Selfishness

Ruling classes consistently impose a way of life that rewards selfishness, creating a *profit economy*. "Profit" means getting more than one gives, and this is widely encouraged in profit economies that *move resources to people who already have them*. The more wealth a person has, the more additional wealth they are able to get.

Capitalism, socialism, and communism are all types of profit economy. Rich people control most of the wealth in capitalism, while the government controls more in socialism and communism.

There are two major kinds of profit economy: market and command. Most unhealthy nations have some mix of both.

Command economies are simple: an authority figure gives an order, and a trapped person obeys the order or gets severely punished. Militaries, chattel slave plantations, and prisons are all command economies. Workers don't choose their bosses, and if workers choose not to work, they receive direct, severe abuse.

Market economies offer more flexibility. Workers can generally choose their boss, choose their type of job, or choose not to work. But unless they are independently wealthy, people who don't work for money face poverty, social isolation, shame, and worse.

While fear of physical punishment motivates workers in command economies, the fear of poverty and low status motivates compliance in market economies. Any form of coerced labor is slavery, and in the 1800s wage jobs were recognized as *wage slavery*.

Whether a lower class person is trying to survive, a middle-class person is trying to keep their comforts, or an entrepreneur is trying to get rich, all of them work for money and so all of them ultimately serve the people with money: the rich and the government which is the source of most money in the first place.

Market economies give wage slaves the flexibility to choose their job, and politicians commonly pretend that this flexibility is the same as freedom. Politicians pretend that the wage slaves live in a free country, and they should be proud and grateful.

Soviet leaders claimed to guarantee citizens' "freedom, democracy, and basic human rights,"[141] while Canadian leadership likewise pretends to care about "defending human rights and democracy."[280] Socialism and capitalism are just different forms of market economy that allow politicians to pretend that the workers are free.

People of healthy nations – who currently or in recent times lived in actual freedom – recognize this truth. Sitting Bull said, "The life of white men is slavery. They are prisoners in their towns or farms."[142] When people must work for others to survive, and are not allowed to choose their own laws nor uphold the laws they obey, widespread selfishness results, and that's what a slave society looks like.

Maintaining Financial Desperation in Market Economies

Authorities use a vast number of techniques to make people feel financially desperate and willing to do work they don't want to do in order to earn money. As a result, many people sacrifice important things like their integrity, health, and family time just to survive.

Different ruling classes manage their economies in different ways in order to maintain desperation and maximize productivity, but there are some common patterns.

Without a job, workers may not be able to pay for housing, food, or health care for their family. Inflation continuously saps the value of previous savings, meaning the money starts to lose value as soon as it is earned. Even relatively well-paid workers often fear not having enough money for retirement, losing a job, or having a health crisis.

Banks and landlords regulate the prices of houses and apartments, calculating the proportion of people's monthly income that they can afford to pay in mortgage or rent. Controlling this debt-to-income ratio means house and rental prices increase at least as much as people's wages, keeping workers from "getting ahead." Property taxes force homeowners to pay to keep the house they already own.

Authorities may make the drawbacks of poverty arbitrarily more terrible, including putting poor people in prison, shaming the poor, forcing them to eat less nutritious food, or taking away their children when they struggle to provide safe, clean homes.

Financial desperation leads to *coerced consent,* where workers who are desperate for money will consent to their own exploitation, each person choosing the least-bad job just to stay alive. People will even beg for a job where they can serve a master because even if they are being exploited, at least they can survive.[226]

In contrast, people of healthy nations have often been called lazy because they only work as hard as needed and no harder. Calling them lazy simultaneously shames them while tricking wage slaves into thinking that endless drudgery is virtuous.[260,19]

Insecurity is common at all levels of wealth. The poor have little money, and they may not know month to month how they will make ends meet. Even the rich feel insecure, knowing that their wealth is the only thing allowing them to live comfortably. With insecurity so widespread, is it any wonder so many people cling to whatever money they can get?

Desperation leads many people to sacrifice their integrity, making it very difficult to have meaningful political conversations. This explains the famous quote from Upton Sinclair: "It is difficult to get a man to understand something, when his salary depends upon his not understanding it."[110]

For example, coal miners commonly refuse to believe in climate change[261], and weapons manufacturers often refuse to consider how governments use their weapons.[6] Intentionally or not, nearly everyone in unhealthy nations supports inappropriate behavior, whether they work for dishonest news media, manufacture goods with toxic materials, or a thousand other ways.

People with integrity face this reality, but few do, as people would recognize that their way of life contributes to big problems in the world, and they might feel the urge to quit their job. But quitting might lead to poverty, perhaps permanently, affecting any family members too. Thus many people say or believe whatever they need to in order to keep the income or wealth they've acquired.

Profit economies make it dangerous to have integrity. Thus it's not just politicians who are corrupt. In one way or another, profit economies corrupt nearly everybody, from the topmost political leaders and business executives to the vast majority of individuals.

Of course, some people have a comfortable life in their profit economy, and maybe you're one of them. If so, do you think this does not pertain to you? Perhaps you like your job, your company has an ethical-sounding mission statement, and you have enough money to survive and even enjoy your days off. Maybe you have money for a rainy day or retirement. Maybe you are sitting pretty.

But consider this. Can you stop? Can you step off your treadmill and quit working for money whenever you please to focus on more meaningful work? And if you did, how long could you keep it up? Unless you have megawealth, some day you would have to return to paid work or face financial desperation. Maybe your friends or family would help you for a while, but sooner or later, you'd likely be in trouble. Unlike those in healthy nations, in the profit economy of an unhealthy nation, you're not surrounded by people who will share food and shelter and ensure your survival needs are met during difficult times.

And if you do have megawealth, you know deep down that you'd better not lose it, or you'll really learn what financial desperation is like.

Perhaps you think that wouldn't happen to you, but the fact that you do not dare step off your job treadmill for very long or risk your retirement savings is proof that you don't want to risk it. Whether we think much about it or not, we are all aware that we must work for money in order to survive and advance in our profit economy.

And therefore the well-off are as trapped as anyone else. The paychecks may vary but the trap is the same. Yes, in a market economy you can choose your job, your boss, and your potential advancement. But the one thing you cannot choose is to not participate. You, just like me and everyone else, are trapped.

Gift Economies Reward and Maintain Generosity

Unlike profit economies that reward selfishness, gift economies reward sharing. To ensure that everyone is taken care of, gift economies move resources to where they are the most needed or where they will do the most good.

I experienced a gift economy among the Ashaninka where sharing food, tools, land, water, and other resources was clearly the norm. Plenty of other people living in other healthy nations, past and present, show that this community-wide and nation-wide sharing is not particularly unusual.

Nancy Basket, a woman of Cherokee descent, summarized the traditional Cherokee culture of sharing this way: "If we all had a lot, then everybody had a lot. If there wasn't a whole lot, then no one had a whole lot."[25]

Ohiyesa of the Sioux described their traditional culture of sharing when he wrote, "During the summer, when Nature is at her best, and provides abundantly for the [Indian], it seems to me that no life is happier than his! Food is free – lodging free – everything free! All were alike rich in the summer, and, again, all were alike poor in the winter and early spring."[67]

Gift economies arise when a whole community or nation embraces the golden rule, each person sharing with the others just as they would want others to share with them.

Gift Economies and Indian Givers

One of my earliest childhood memories involves giving somebody a gift and noticing that they didn't use it. When I tried to take it back, I was called an "Indian giver." To be a generous gift-giver, I was supposed to release all interest in what happens to my gift after I give it. The gift becomes someone else's property and therefore is no longer any of my business.

Wanting to avoid the scorn of being called an Indian giver, that's how I learned to give gifts – first it belonged to me, and now it belongs to someone else. It took decades for me to learn that this attitude towards sharing is rooted in private property ownership and essential to maintaining authoritarian nations. It turns out that my younger self had the healthier attitude to gift-giving.

In gift economies, people take responsibility to learn where gifts are most needed or valued, and everyone helps circulate gifts until they get to that highest use. This is where the derogatory phrase "Indian giver" comes from: people of North American healthy nations (known as Indians) sometimes gave gifts to European colonists, noticed they weren't being used, and thus asked for them back so the gifts could be given elsewhere. European colonists thus saw "Indian giving" as a violation of their private property rights.

Nancy Basket described how the Europeans commonly misunderstood the Cherokee gift economy: "We would know each other well enough to see what they might need. And if we would give somebody a gift and they didn't use it, we would be embarrassed. And we would either take it back or something else because it wasn't being used. She didn't need it. And people called us Indian givers for that."[25]

"Indian giver" became a negative label for someone who gave a gift and now selfishly wants it back. In reality, they are behaving thoughtfully, noticing whether the gift is needed. If the gift goes unused, the so-called Indian giver exerts extra effort to retrieve the unused item and give it to someone else who needs it more.

Gift-economy practices can seem offensive to people in profit economies, and profit-economy practices can seem offensive to people in gift economies.

A person in a gift economy may feel upset if a person accepts a gift, doesn't use it, and then refuses to pass it on to someone else. A person from a profit economy may feel upset if they receive a gift only to find that the giver wants it back. Both sides may feel offended, and it reflects a fundamentally different perspective on sharing (and trusting others to share) versus hoarding (and not trusting others to share). Do gifts keep moving until they arrive where they are most needed? Or do people hoard possessions whether they need them or not?

Potawatomi woman Robin Kimmerer noted the consequences when she wrote, "If all the world is a commodity, how poor we grow. When all the world is a gift in motion, how wealthy we become."[128]

This attitude to gift-giving stems from the deep recognition that all of life is simply the giving of divine gifts. Every spider, bear, bush, and cloud is giving its sacred gifts and somehow contributing to the web of life. Who would want to stop all that giving? Gift economies aim to circulate gifts rather than hoard them, and this kind of human economy fits in well with the larger nonhuman economy of all life.

When whole nations embrace a gift economy, their way of life benefits the living world. When humans form reciprocal relationships with nonhumans, giving to the plant and animal communities while gratefully receiving enough to live, the whole ecosystem benefits from the humans' presence.

Gift economies have many practical benefits. They move resources from the haves to the have-nots, minimizing inequality. They ensure neighbors take care of each other. People might face scarcity together occasionally, but nobody suffers poverty alone while others have abundance. Gift economies help people take care of each other whenever a big challenge arises.

Gift economies also make it easier to develop and keep one's integrity. When a person isn't afraid of poverty, it becomes easier to face reality, even when it's unpleasant.

When everybody is expected to stand for what's right, this is the way of life that results – a life of shared abundance. As Okanagan woman Jeannette Armstrong said, *"The realization that people and community are there to sustain you creates the most secure feeling in the world..."*[183]

In unhealthy nations where a few people dominate the rest and authorities forbid people from seeking justice and upholding their own laws, most people are left trying to survive and get as comfortable as possible. Widespread selfishness is the result.

But it doesn't have to be this way. Individuals, communities, and whole nations are capable of generosity when everyone stands for a culture of mutual respect, and nobody rules over anybody else.

Revolutionary Activity #10
Give first

How can you form new friendships where sharing is the norm? Someone needs to give first to start a relationship of generous reciprocity.

Think of three ways you could give something to a total stranger, not knowing or caring whether they would respond generously. For example, you could mentor a child or make a nutritious meal for someone who's sick or recovering from childbirth. Without any expectation of return, give to strangers in ways that, even if the relationship ended immediately, it would be ok. Notice which people show gratitude and give back in their own ways over time, and what relationships of reciprocity form.

When I was 12, I was in the lunch line in school, and a boy ahead of me discovered he didn't have money. I didn't know him, but I offered to buy him lunch, and he became one of my best friends. This taught me to give first before I've received anything, and just see what happens.

Revolutionary Activity #11
Receive graciously to have reciprocity over time

Trading and bartering don't involve generosity because they are even exchanges in the moment. When you receive someone's gift and try to make it an equal exchange by giving them something, you're not acknowledging their generosity and allowing your gratitude to grow. You're essentially receiving the object but rejecting the generosity behind it.

Next time someone does something kind for you, just say thanks and enjoy receiving the gift. Whether they're giving you a compliment, making you a meal, or anything else, do not try to give back something of equal value in the moment. Instead, let your feeling of gratitude grow and trust that you'll find ways to give back in reciprocity over time. If you do want to give the other person something, clarify that you're also giving a gift and not making a trade.

Chapter 8: Why Don't More People Stand Together?

A human nation is a living organism. And just like a tree or lion or ant colony, a human nation can become injured.

Any disrespect between two people is a type of cultural injury, not just a personal concern. Nancy Basket says, "If there is trouble in a family, the whole nation suffers."[25] Martin Luther King Jr echoed this when he wrote, "Injustice anywhere is a threat to justice everywhere."[136]

Like all living organisms, injured human nations try to heal themselves. Healthy human nations heal their wounds of disrespectful behavior by deeply addressing the trouble and bringing back a baseline of mutual respect. This is the essence of cultural healing.

Human nations become unhealthy when they are blocked from healing by rich and powerful people who benefit from disrespecting and exploiting their neighbors. These people selfishly resist returning to that respectful baseline that humans find so fundamentally satisfying.

Rulers and other authorities in positions of power would clearly lose their current ability to dominate and exploit everyone else if their unhealthy nation were to change. Thus they use their wealth and power to make sure the unhealthy nation and all its deep disrespect continue.

What are common ways that rulers and lower authorities prevent cultural healing, blocking people from standing together in solidarity to collectively stop injustices? And what can people do to intentionally generate a nation that maximizes solidarity and encourages deep respect for all?

Sabotaging Solidarity in Unhealthy Nations

Authorities and wealthy people sabotage solidarity in many ways.

Attacking our Spiritual Leaders

"Spirituality" is simply how a person relates to themselves and the world, and spiritual leaders help people relate to the world in a good way. A spiritual leader is anyone who helps their people confront troubles like injustice, corruption, selfishness, confusion, shame, poverty, low self-worth, and disconnection from the Earth. Spiritual leaders commonly help people share, build up their self-worth and dignity, help them reconnect with the Earth, and remind them that they have a proud ancestry as they bring people together to confront injustices.

The modern-day term for spiritual leader is "social activist." Whether they are called "social activists" or "spiritual leaders," they are the ones who show the most bravery, wisdom, and generosity as they bring people together to confront injustice. Unfortunately, because spiritual leaders confront the oppression that benefits the wealthy and powerful, selfish authorities commonly attack them and undermine their efforts.

Authorities around the world have found many ways to attack social activists, the spiritual leaders most willing to confront injustice in their unhealthy nation.

In the mid-1900s, East German police developed a practice called *Zersetzung,* meaning disintegration or decomposition. This police practice drove activists to mentally, emotionally, and socially disintegrate without any explicit use of force. The police arranged for various government bureaucracies to lose citizens' forms, take longer than usual to respond to citizens' inquiries or requests, or otherwise seriously frustrate the lives of activists. East German police would sabotage people's reputation. They fabricated and circulated love letters or evidence of illegal behavior among an activist's friends and family in order to sabotage relationships, and they often succeeded.[258]

They also surveilled activists to dig up and publicize any private behaviors they might want hidden, such as drug use or criminal records. They might make appointments or order goods in the activist's name. They would even manipulate a person's home, secretly entering and rearranging items like clothes and only removing things no burglar would snatch, such as a single piece of important mail. They might secretly damage a bike or car. Activists would start to doubt their memory and their ability to live a functional life. Police might cause strange noises on a phone line, repeatedly stop and search someone, and make conspicuous visits to the activist's workplace so coworkers would be aware of the police's interest. People's careers were ruined without them even understanding why. Zersetzung was gaslighting on a massive scale.[100,108,258]

Can you imagine what it would be like if the government deliberately made your life as difficult as possible, just because you confronted injustices with your neighbors?

There are many other examples of this kind of bureaucratic assault, including reputation sabotage. For instance, in the 2010s the US decided to have Julian Assange accused of sexual assault in Sweden after Assange revealed huge numbers of war crimes and deceit by US political leaders. The original Swedish prosecutor Eva Finne acknowledged, "There is no suspicion of any crime whatsoever." However, corrupt politics won out, and continual political persecution resulted in Assange being trapped for over a decade in an embassy and later a British prison.[48]

Authorities may also audit the taxes of activists to force them to waste huge amounts of time. In 2022, American Matt Taibbi exposed documents showing how the US government pressured a social media company to censor content, and the US federal tax authority (IRS) opened an investigation of him. Fortunately, powerful politicians contacted the IRS on Taibbi's behalf, and the IRS agents decided Taibbi didn't owe any taxes after all.[189]

Authorities may also take a more direct approach to thwarting social activism: murder the activists. Famous social activists include Jesus Christ and Martin Luther King Jr. Jesus Christ consistently broke the law to feed[75] and heal[76] people who needed it, and he even attacked moneylenders for profiting in the Temple.[134] He associated with Zealots, known for resisting Roman rule, including having at least one Zealot among his disciples.[86,58] He kept serving his people in the most meaningful ways he could, knowing he would be killed for it.[135,193] Finally the authorities arrested and nailed him to a cross and left him to die in public along with two other revolutionaries. It was normal for Roman authorities to publicly torture revolutionaries to death with crucifixion in order to scare everyone else into submission.[58]

The death of Martin Luther King Jr offers another example. King lead or supported many civil rights efforts in the United States to improve the treatment of black people in the 1950s and 1960s.[139] Over time, he also took a stand against imperialism, acknowledging the hypocrisy of the US attacking the Vietnamese while claiming to value democracy.[137] Like Jesus Christ, King carried on his work fully knowing it would cost him his life, even acknowledging this in a speech the night before his assassination.[138]

On April 4, 1968, a sniper murdered Martin Luther King Jr. The government arrested and convicted James Earl Ray for this act, but a great deal of evidence indicated that someone else had actually killed Martin Luther King Jr.[61]

In the following decades, activists gathered copious evidence that the US government had killed Martin Luther King Jr, and they presented their case at a civil trial in Memphis, Tennessee in 1999. Because they could not sue government officials directly, King's family sued a private citizen named Loyd Jowers as well as "Other Unknown Co-conspirators." Loyd Jowers had admitted he was involved in King's death, and these "unknown" co-conspirators were the police and intelligence agencies that couldn't be sued directly in court. The purpose of the trial was for the King family to publicly share evidence that intelligence agencies and federal and local police conspired to execute Martin Luther King Jr.[61]

Trial evidence showed that the defendant, Jowers, had said in a recorded meeting that he had helped plan King's death with the Memphis police department. Several witnesses testified that the sniper was on the ground, not in a balcony as the police claimed, and police never gathered these witnesses' testimony. The scope on the supposed murder weapon was not sighted, so as judge Joe Brown said, it "literally could not have hit the broadside of a barn." Also metallurgical tests indicated that the bullet which killed King had a different metallic composition than those in James Earl Ray's supposed murder weapon.[61]

The civil trial court ruled in favor of the Kings, agreeing that the evidence indicated that Jowers and "Unknown Co-conspirators" had indeed killed Martin Luther King Jr.[61]

Attacking Groups

The Nazis worked diligently to scare Germans into submission in the 1930s. Bruce Bettelheim described how a group of activist lawyers objected to various Nazi policies, and so the German police arrested all their leaders.[27]

This led to group members believing they were safe as long as they stayed out of leadership positions. The Nazis did not want any public opposition, so they began arresting lawyers essentially randomly across the group to scare everybody into submission. Nobody was explicitly told why they were arrested, but they all learned in prison that it was due to their activism work. The Nazis left a few leading lawyers in place when this was useful to them.[27]

Infiltration is particularly devious, where undercover police officers or contractors will pretend to be activists and participate in social movements. In 2011, eight British women activists filed a lawsuit stating they were tricked into having long-term relationships with police who sabotaged their efforts to reduce animal cruelty and pollution going back to the 1980s. Prosecutors and police chiefs set up 12 "inquiries" to investigate police misconduct, but all took place in secret and there has been no sign of change. Some of the women even had children with the undercover police who had secretly undermined all the good work they were doing.[78]

The Tsarist Russian secret police provide more examples of police infiltration. Helpful informants were more likely to get into university or get a job, while incorruptible activists were denied. One police chief even allowed infiltrators to engage in illegal behavior to earn the trust of the real activists. Infiltrators were trained in all the fashionable revolutionary and socialist theories, and whenever an activist group seemed to settle on one theory, the infiltrators would start advocating for an opposing one, never letting the group settle on a coherent understanding of their problems and what to do about them. The manipulation ran deep![53,16]

These techniques are all devious, but they're still far from ideal for authorities. Ideally activists would never start their own groups, but would join organizations secretly run by the rich and powerful where they can be most easily surveilled and controlled.

People who benefit from injustice sabotage efforts to stop it.

Astroturf Social Movements

Authorities may also start their own *astroturf social movements*, groups of organizations that claim to be grassroots but are actually controlled by the authorities from the start. If there were no social justice movement, angry people might start their own and it might become revolutionary. But if authorities could create their own social movement they secretly control, activists might join it and invest huge amounts of time and energy into a movement which only sets moderate goals and does not achieve deep change.

As one example from the early 1900s, secret police in Tsarist Russia secretly started trade unions that acted as if they were independent. Many thousands of workers joined, excited to be part of a movement for better wages and better working conditions. S. V.

Zubatov, a secret police chief, had the "movement leaders" host pro-monarchy classes so that workers would think of the Russian monarch as supportive and wise rather than selfish. The unions would pretend to negotiate with factory owners about wage increases, while the real negotiations were happening between the factory owners and the police chief.[16,101]

Tens of thousands of workers joined Russian labor unions secretly controlled by the police, thinking they were all coming together to seek meaningful change. The workers legitimately wanted that change and worked hard for it, not knowing that the leadership was directing their energy in a way that they would only see moderate improvements at best.[101]

Imagine if you spent hundreds of hours supporting such a labor movement, tired of the poor wages, long hours, and dangerous work environments. How would you feel if you discovered later that it was being manipulated by the most powerful people in your society to prevent meaningful change?

A similar manipulation is playing out in the United States with the Black Lives Matter movement. In 2024, the "impact" page on blacklivesmatter.com proclaimed "We are building an institution to fight white supremacy."[105] The "about us" page on m4bl.org (Movement for Black Lives) stated "We are anti-capitalist."[5] Yet the movement is heavily funded by some of the wealthiest white capitalists on the planet, including the people behind the Ford Foundation who donated more than $840,000,000 to Black Lives Matter-related organizations between 2011 and 2021.[85]

The Ford Foundation is the "philanthropic" organization based on the wealth of white capitalist Henry Ford, founder of the Ford car company. As early as 1951 it had ties with the US Central Intelligence Agency (CIA), which requested its help doing psychological warfare operations in Asia.[59] With this background in psychological warfare, the Ford Foundation already had experience deceiving and manipulating whole societies in service of US imperialism. Do you think it might use the same manipulative techniques in the US, further refined after decades of practice?

The Ford Foundation was already known in the 1960s and 1970s for funding "moderate" political groups to try and attract black people away from revolutionary movements like the Black Panthers.[293]

Ford Foundation directors have included some of the most politically connected American capitalists, including John McCloy who also worked as president of the World Bank, high commissioner for Occupied Germany after World War II, assistant secretary of war, and chairman of Chase Manhattan Bank.[264] Other rich donors to Black Lives Matter-related groups include multi-billionaires Mark Zuckerberg[3] (ceo of Facebook) and Pierre Omidyar[4] (cofounder of eBay).

Just as the vast majority of activists in the astroturf Russian labor unions legitimately wanted change, many well-meaning activists have supported Black Lives Matter. But sadly, the most influential people – the funders and their choice of organizations and leaders they fund – have found ways to direct that activist energy to effectively seek only moderate change and avert deep change.

After 10 years, what was there to show? Many wealthy and powerful people implemented superficial changes that might feel rewarding and give the appearance that Black Lives Matter was making progress, but which do not end the oppression of black people. The government announced a new federal holiday called Juneteenth in honor of the end of chattel slavery. Companies like Zoom and Google allow people to choose their skin color in their profiles. Some large news companies and publishers have decided to go all-out by capitalizing the letter "b" when writing about black people.[174] Wow, what progress!

Many companies include (or used to include) some variation of "diversity, equity, and inclusion" projects geared towards helping employees work productively together. Corporate officers that claim to oppose racism commonly discuss microaggressions that hurt an individual's feelings but do not address the massive macroaggressions which generate systems of prison slavery.[1]

What are those macroaggressions that a grassroots liberation movement might inspire people to fight against?

Consider the real mechanisms keeping black people oppressed in the United States. When police spend extra time patrolling poor black neighborhoods and black people get longer prison sentences than whites for the same offense, black people end up spending much more time in prison than white people for the same crimes.[227]

Corrupt higher authorities encourage corruption in the police. Police whistleblowers who call out corruption consistently risk losing their careers, and sometimes their lives.[231]

Many police officers commit perjury in court when it suits them and commonly get away with it, as found in repeated academic studies spanning decades and acknowledged by many police officers, judges, and lawyers themselves in interviews, meaning that the legal system knowingly tolerates false evidence.[231] Police deceit is so common that they have their own term for it: "testilying," a combination of "testify" and "lying."[94] Studies show that 98% of federal prisoners plea-bargain, meaning they are threatened with such long prison sentences that they plead guilty in exchange for a shorter sentence. Plea bargaining sends people to prison whether or not they are actually guilty without going to trial.[116]

Federal prisoner surveys in 2008 showed that prison sexual assault is so rampant that, when combined with sexual assault rates outside of prison, there are more male-victim sexual assaults than female-victim in the United States.[229] Prisoners cannot legally choose not to work, and even if they could legally decline, prison administrators commonly violate the law with impunity, meaning they would force prisoners to work whether it was legal or not.[232]

John Ehrlichman was White House counsel in the Nixon administration, and he admitted that the whole "war on drugs," which has sent millions of people to prison, was implemented specifically to persecute people who opposed the rulers' oppressive policies. He told a reporter in 1994, "the Nixon White House... had two enemies: the antiwar left and black people... We knew we couldn't make it illegal to be either against the [Vietnam] war or black, but by getting the public to associate the hippies with marijuana and blacks with heroin, and then criminalizing both heavily, we could disrupt those communities. We could arrest their leaders, raid their homes, break up their meetings, and vilify them night after night on the evening news. Did we know we were lying about the drugs? Of course we did."[26]

This would be bad enough if drug use were a terrible crime that could only be stopped by imprisoning people, but researchers find that drug-treatment programs reduce both drug-use and crime more than imprisonment. In fact, research shows that going to prison increases drug use.[28,287,273] Because a core purpose of the "war on drugs" is to persecute activists and the poor, authorities consistently ignore this research.[26]

This is what prison slavery looks like in the United States right now: vast numbers of black people (and people from other groups, mostly poor) are in prison without having a fair trial, are often persecuted by dishonest police and judges who knowingly tolerate perjury, are forced to work, are commonly threatened with sexual assault, and given disproportionately long sentences. And all because of activities that, in many cases such as drug possession, shouldn't be considered crimes in the first place.

How would you feel if you were unjustly trapped in such an abusive prison system? How would you feel if your parent or sibling or child were trapped, and you couldn't see them day after day for years or decades?

How do you feel knowing that if you worked with others to free unjustly imprisoned people, such as by confronting the responsible politicians, judges, police, or prison wardens, you would be punished? Even prison reform-activists can only ask authorities to pursue justice. They're not allowed to directly seek justice themselves, as any interference with the legal system is strictly forbidden and heavily punished. This is what it means to live in an unfree society – you're stuck with unjust laws which are unfairly enforced, like the war on drugs, and you would be punished for seeking justice.

This oppression profoundly benefits the rich, as it discourages and disrupts the deep solidarity needed to end the injustices black people face in so many areas of life. Thus the rich keep getting richer while many black people and other disadvantaged groups remain in relative poverty.

Black Lives Matter organizers proclaim they are anti-white supremacy and anti-capitalist. But do you think that a movement so heavily funded by rich white capitalists will end the oppression that benefits them so much?

Black Lives Matter isn't the only astroturf movement in the United States. For example, the multibillionaire Koch brothers have spent over $160 million to fund at least 90 "independent" research and opinion organizations to trick people into thinking climate change is fake – all to protect their investment in their oil and chemical company.[140]

Creating and controlling astroturf social movements is common in unhealthy nations where a few powerful people control vast wealth and work to keep it at any cost.

Whether attacking activists, undermining social movements, or sponsoring astroturf social groups, authorities selfishly work to undermine solidarity in order to maintain the status quo. If people wanted to create a nation without this deep selfishness, how might they do this?

Revolutionary Activity #12
Channel your anger

How do you feel reading about such profound corruption in the "justice system"? How do you feel knowing that, since you live in an unfree, unhealthy nation, you would be punished if you confronted legal authorities to seek real justice for the prisoners?

If you feel anger or other difficult feelings reading about this, that's ok. The energy behind those feelings is a gift; it's the energy that can motivate you to help stand for real justice. Remember that you're not alone, and plenty of people want justice just like you. Find a productive way to channel that energy, such as by confronting injustices where you live, educating others, or helping found a new healthy nation where people would never tolerate such abuses.

A Case Study in Creating a Society that Chooses Generous Servant-Leaders: The Haudenosaunee

Imagine living in a society where the leaders are the most generous, and where the leaders encourage deep solidarity and connection instead of sabotaging it. Imagine a society where activists who confront injustice are rewarded with gratitude instead of punishment.

This is not a fantasy, but the normal way people live in healthy nations during traditional times. The Haudenosaunee's traditional leaders were their spiritual leaders, and were expected to be extremely generous. Leaders "act more as conduits of the will of the people than as independent representatives of the people,"[207] and "when they don't perform, the will of the people will remove them."[182]

What sort of society would have the spiritual strength to choose leaders like this, and to replace any leader who does not live up to their standards?

Long ago, several nations in eastern North America were suffering from a long period of violence, and eventually they decided to create a confederacy to ensure lasting peace. This became known as the Haudenosaunee Confederacy, also known as the Iroquois, which has survived as a healthy nation for over 900 years.[114]

In their book *Basic Call to Consciousness,* Haudenosaunee writers summarized many crucial aspects of their society. It is impossible to briefly recount all the ways the Haudenosaunee have maintained a healthy nation for so long, but I believe these elements have many lessons to teach:

1. *Solidarity:* As one people, they stand in solidarity to ensure that if anyone is attacked, the entire Confederacy would respond.[205,206]

    Everyone is trained from birth to uphold the agreements of their society, and to defend anyone who is oppressed. They did not just make a strong government to keep them safe. Recognizing that "universal justice is the product of a spiritually strong society," they raise children to be spiritually strong adults who accept responsibility for upholding rules that work for everyone.[208]

2. *Intentionally Avoiding Causes of Past Conflicts:* The founders studied causes of past conflicts and created a Grand Council that helped resolve disputes, among other functions.[204]

3. *Acknowledging the Earth's Needs:* The Haudenosaunee take the nonhumans' needs into account. They embrace strict laws of conservation and carefully avoid degrading the land.[201]

As a result, in traditional times the Haudenosaunee lived with an "almost unimaginable abundance... of nuts, berries, roots, and herbs... the rivers teemed with fish and the forest and its meadows abounded with game..."[201]

4. *Achieving Peace by Standing for Justice:* When there is no justice, "peace" is actually submission. The Haudenosaunee's founders prioritized justice, saying that "if absolute justice was established in the world, peace would naturally follow."[201] They even prioritized justice over rigid rules, noting "the society was founded on concepts of moral justice, not statute law."[207]

5. *Rejecting Private Property:* The Haudenosaunee wisely reject private property and emphasize sharing. They wrote, "That idea (property) would produce slavery...[and] would destroy our culture, which requires that every individual live in service to the Spiritual Ways and The People."[202] They established the rule that "no one has a right to a greater share of the wealth of society than anyone else."[207]

Since the Haudenosaunee avoid selfishness, they do not need to fear anybody mooching off others' hard work and generosity.

6. *Avoiding Conquering Other People:* The founders committed to never impose taxes, religion, or any injustice on anyone they defeated in war. While the Haudenosaunee were willing to keep fighting a war until the threat was fully addressed, adversaries could call for a cessation of hostilities at any time. They

committed to never have a society where a few people ruled over the rest, even when they won the war and could be the rulers![206]

7. *Leaders Serve the People:* They avoid factions,[204] and no unaccountable leaders impose laws on anyone. Their leaders are expected to be generous.[201]

What was the end result of a society based in part on these principles? Whereas one encyclopedia defines a "utopia" as "impossibly idealistic"[263], the Haudenosaunee writers described how, prior to the arrival of European unhealthy nations, "It was, in fact, a kind of Utopia, a place where no one went hungry, a place where the people were happy and healthy."[201]

Even centuries ago, the Haudenosaunee sometimes went through hard times such as famines or wars. This shows that living in a utopia doesn't mean life is easy. It means that you can trust the people around you to take care of each other when challenges arise.

These principles show the importance of spiritual strength and what it means to live in a free society. When everyone in a nation has the spiritual strength to stand for what's right, each person will expect everyone else to likewise have that strength. And when everybody is expected to stand for justice, then justice and mutual respect become normal, and that's what a free society looks like.

Part 3 offers a practical path to begin building a healthy nation, starting with cultivating your spiritual strength and forming new healthy communities where people hold each other to high standards of good behavior so that integrity and generosity become normal, and trust is pervasive.

Not everyone will want to walk this path, but you can find people who do. As healthy communities form, they will be the building blocks of future healthy nations that embrace a respectful way of life among the people, and between the people and the Earth.

Chapter 9: Why Do People Obey Corrupt Leaders?

The common experience of living in a nation dominated by a ruling class comes down to this: you must obey their laws whether you like them or not. And even if you like their laws, you must not do anything yourself to enforce those laws when someone else violates them. Responding to bad behavior can only be done by enforcement agents chosen by the ruling class, called the police. If you take action on your own to pursue justice when someone behaves badly, you risk being punished. Whether or not you like the rulers and lower authorities, you must obey.

Obeying corrupt, unaccountable leaders is considered normal in unhealthy nations. People don't choose their bosses at work, don't choose their commanders in the military, and don't really choose their political leaders. In democracies, politicians run and win based primarily on money, and therefore they are effectively chosen by the rich.

How on Earth do so many people think it is OK to obediently follow the rules of corrupt leaders? How did people get to the point where they submissively obey laws they don't agree with and corrupt authorities they don't like, and then accept their own obedience as legitimate and normal?

Nearly all religious and political authorities insist on and promote obedience. To make obedience seem normal and right, they have purposely hidden or distorted important aspects of history by controlling the contents of holy books like the Bible, Torah, and Quran, as well as history books and other teaching materials, and emphasized the aspects that promote obedience.

No example better reveals how this distortion works than the real story of history's most misunderstood spiritual leader: Jesus Christ.

What Would Jesus Do? We Have Been Purposely Trained Not To Know

For almost 2,000 years, Christian authorities have taught Christian followers to be obedient, and to see Jesus Christ as an example of righteous obedience.

One elder of the Church of Jesus Christ of Latter Day Saints claims, "Jesus Christ, the Only Begotten Son of God, learned perfect obedience."[256] A Catholic leader claims, "Christ asks for our obedience in many ways."[214] An Evangelical Christian pastor wrote, "Jesus Christ came as the incarnated divine Son to live a human life of perfect obedience and submission."[173]

However, the Bible shows that Jesus Christ was anything but obedient. To really understand Jesus, we must understand the times he lived in.

The Romans had conquered Jerusalem and the surrounding region about 60 years before Jesus was born. They imposed heavy taxes, unwanted imperialism, a client king that obeyed Roman authorities, and generally treated the people abusively. Many Jewish revolutionaries worked to free themselves from the Romans, longing for a country where Jews could be safe. Eventually this led to a series of wars between the Romans and the rebellious Jews, starting with the First Jewish Revolt in 66 CE, about 30 years after Jesus' death.[155]

Thus, during Jesus' time, oppressed Jewish people longed for a "messiah," which means "savior" or "liberator."[175] It's easy to understand why. The Jews wanted a revolutionary leader to help save them from oppressive Roman rule.

Jesus Christ saw huge amounts of needless suffering all around. A few people were rich and had far more than they needed, and many suffered needlessly from troubles like hunger, sickness, and poverty.

Instead of merely obeying the law and tolerating these troubles, Christ consistently stood for what's right *even in violation of the law*. He had the spiritual strength to stand for what's right at great personal risk, knowing he would die for serving his people.

Consider how incredibly disobedient Jesus Christ was:

- *Fed people illegally:* Jesus Christ illegally fed hungry people on the Sabbath. (Mark 2:23-24)[75]

- *Healed people illegally:* Christ illegally healed people on the Sabbath. (Matthew 12:10, Mark 3:2)[197,196]

- *Prioritized doing the right thing over following unjust laws:* When religious and legal authorities reminded him of the law, Christ said, "The Sabbath was made for man, not man for the Sabbath." (Mark 2:27)[195] In other words, when people are in need and the law prevents helping them, we should prioritize doing the right thing and helping each other over following an unjust law. Christ's attitude is similar to the Haudenosaunee's, whose nation was "founded on concepts of moral justice, not statute law."[207]

- *Attacked predatory money lenders:* Jesus physically attacked predatory moneylenders (the equivalent to today's bankers and payday loan sharks) in the Temple who exploited his people. (Mark 11:15-18)[74]

- *Associated with other revolutionaries:* Christ associated with Zealots, and at least one of his disciples was a Zealot. Zealots were revolutionaries. Among other things, Zealots were known for not paying taxes and even killing Roman tax collectors.[86,58]

- *At trial, Jesus was accused of challenging Roman authority:* At his trial, among other things, Christ was accused of subverting the nation, encouraging illegal tax avoidance, and claiming he was the rightful leader of the Jews.[133] He did not deny the charges.[77]

- *Christ was killed like a revolutionary:* The two men killed with Christ were not just thieves. They were revolutionaries.[58] They were nailed to a cross and publicly left to die. The Romans used crucifixion to scare others away from revolutionary activities.

Christ stood up for his people against oppressive authorities in worldly and spiritual ways, seeking to free them from Roman rule. He was publicly tortured to death to scare others away from having the spiritual strength to stand for what's right because the Roman government didn't want people to stand for what's right – they wanted people to obey, and so they tried to scare the public into submission.

Some Christians claim that Christ was obedient because he said, "Give back to Caesar what is Caesar's," suggesting people should pay their taxes.[194] But revolutionaries commonly debate whether to pay taxes. Should you pay taxes to avoid government harassment, so you can focus on liberating your people? Or do you choose not to pay taxes to a corrupt government and face the consequences? Christ clearly was one of these revolutionaries who chose to pay taxes while seeking to liberate his people.

Unfortunately for the Roman authorities, Jesus was extremely inspirational, and a religion formed that continued to spread his teachings after he died. The revolutionary movement also continued, with a series of Jewish-Roman rebellions occurring between 66 and 135 CE. None were successful.[86]

The religion inspired by Jesus Christ kept spreading, and by the 300s CE, multiple sects existed. Finally, in 380 CE, something strange happened. The same Roman government that had killed Jesus Christ imposed Christianity as a religion on the Roman Empire, requiring people to worship Jesus Christ as their spiritual leader. Why?[216]

Instead of allowing revolutionary forms of Christianity to spread and inspire more people to become revolutionaries like Christ, the Roman emperor embraced it, but he embraced a specific version of Christianity *that trained people for obedience*. The Roman state trained Christian followers to think of themselves as lambs, to think of Jesus as obedient, and to think obedience is good.

When Roman emperor Theodosius imposed *his* version of Christianity on the Roman Empire, he said those who did not accept it were "demented and insane" and those who would not obey the new religion "shall be smitten first by divine vengeance and secondly by the retribution of our own initiative." Anyone who disagreed with the official Roman version of Christianity was threatened with severe punishment.[216]

In many ways, the Roman state spread a religious ideology that *discouraged the spiritual strength* needed to stand up for what's right. Thus Christians were trained to *misunderstand their revolutionary spiritual leader Jesus Christ,* even while authorities required them to worship Christ, a man of incredible spiritual strength.

As a result, Christians have endlessly debated when to obey, how to obey, or whom to obey. But *the attitude of obedience itself is rarely questioned,* which is why every Christian society in history has had oppressive authorities that Christians have obeyed. And whenever Christians have had a revolution, they merely put different oppressive authorities in charge that likewise expect obedience.

So how exactly did Roman emperor Theodosius impose a version of Christianity that discouraged spiritual strength and encouraged obedience instead? It turns out that ruling classes around the world want to train people to obey corrupt authorities, and they commonly use similar tricks.

To understand these tricks, I invite you to step into the shoes of a ruler and ask, "if I were a ruler, how would I train people for obedience?"

Ancient and Modern Religious Training to Maintain Submissive Obedience

If you were a king, and you wanted to train your subjects to obey you, what would you do? For starters, you would want to train your subjects to not stand for justice, and instead to passively accept your laws and how you choose to enforce them (or not).

And what would be a highly effective way of accomplishing that? How about imposing a religion that trained your subjects to believe that obeying authorities was good and morally right, and disobeying was evil and bad?

Every religion has aspects of wisdom and beauty. However, when ruling classes impose an ideology or religion, they consistently twist or distort this ancient wisdom and beauty so that people learn to submit to authorities instead of personally standing for what's right. Unfortunately, this is essentially how religions like Christianity, Islam, and Buddhism train people for submissive obedience.

Roman emperor Theodosius imposed *his* version of Christianity on ancient Rome, and he threatened severe punishment to anyone who didn't convert.[216] And what does the official Christian Bible say? According to 1-Peter 2:13: "Submit yourselves for the Lord's sake to every human authority: whether to the emperor, as the supreme authority, or to governors…"[190]

Islamic rulers have also propagated this same pro-obedience ideology in their religion. The Quran says, "O believers! Obey Allah and obey the Messenger and those in authority among you."[271] Other authoritarian religions also train people to believe that God says to obey their rulers.

The trouble runs deeper though. In abusive relationships, the abuser will often try to control the victim by lowering the victim's self-esteem in various ways – by making them doubt themselves and doubt their own senses, by shaming and belittling them, by training the victim to think they're lucky to live with the abuser and would be worse off on their own. Victims may be told that abuse is normal in relationships, or victims deserve what they get. Not surprisingly, victims who believe these things are more likely to tolerate abuse and stay in abusive relationships instead of leaving them.

Unhealthy nations all have a ruling class that exploits the rest, so all unhealthy nations create and maintain massive, multi-generational abusive relationships. The rulers are the ultimate oppressive abusers, with many lower authorities in religion, business, and politics also abusing or exploiting others.

In unhealthy nations – just like in abusive domestic relationships between two people – abusive authorities commonly impose ideologies that encourage things like shame, low self-worth, disconnection from divinity, fear of one's core instincts, rejection of pleasure, sexism, beliefs that humans are inherently selfish and untrustworthy, and beliefs that people deserve to suffer.

Self-respecting people do not passively submit to abusive authorities, but when people deeply embrace these hurtful attitudes or beliefs, they can become more willing to accept abuse, isolation, dissatisfaction, apathy, meaninglessness, superficiality, or despair.

For example, the Catholic Church's official dogma states that humans are "inclined to sin" and have "an inclination to evil." Still one of the most followed religions in the world, Catholicism states that the first human (Adam) "lost the original holiness and justice he had received from God, not only for himself but for all human beings."[43,45]

And it's not just humans who are inherently bad or evil. Catholic dogma states that human sin "put the world as a whole in the sinful condition."[44]

This message that humans are born without holiness, inclined to evil, and disconnected from divinity is deeply shameful and discouraging. And it gets worse – apparently we were born into a sinful world that our sinful ways helped create! What message could possibly encourage more hopelessness?[45,44]

The Islamic Quran likewise causes people to doubt their own sense of right and wrong, and to trust authorities instead. The Quran repeatedly states Allah's omniscience: "Surely Allah is Almighty, All-Wise[268]... And Allah is All-Hearing, All-Knowing."[269] The Quran paints the Islamic God Allah as omniscient, and how should a person respond if they have a feeling, urge, or thought that does not align with their authorities' religious text? The Quran is clear: "Perhaps you dislike something which is good for you and like something which is bad for you. Allah knows and you do not know."[267]

Buddhist authorities have pulled the same authority-supporting tricks. Visitors to Tibet prior to the Chinese takeover in the 1950s found Tibetan Buddhists teaching that the world is full of evil. Every bend of the road, stream crossing, or village entrance had to have a row of flags to exorcize evil spirits. Lakes, wells, and streams teamed with demons who brought floods and hail storms upon anyone who violated their religious leaders' rules.[143]

Evil could exist almost anywhere, from doorways to cracks in stones, and – surprise, surprise – only the priests could protect people from evil, for a fee of course. This ideology scared people away from the wilderness, seeing nonhumans as evil spirits rather than teachers and siblings offering their gifts. This further trained people to live in fear and kept them in poverty.[143]

Even the Tibetan Buddhist belief in karma has been used to excuse extreme exploitation by rich monks and lamas. The fourteenth dalai lama implied that serfs clearly deserve their suffering when he said, "A poor Tibetan was less inclined to envy or resent his Tibetan landlord because he knew that each of them was reaping the seed he had sown in his previous life."[88]

Why would rulers deliberately push these attitudes and beliefs? Do you think it's a coincidence that these attitudes and beliefs discourage the spiritual strength and collective solidarity that might allow people to free themselves by uniting, making their own respectful laws, and upholding those laws together?

This may seem like a stretch, but it is no coincidence that rulers train people for submissive obedience. Sadly there is even more evidence to back this up.

Authoritarian religions also tend to discourage deep sensual pleasure, and Buddhism offers a clear example. The Buddha laid out the Four Noble Truths. Of these, the second is the Noble Truth of the Cause of Suffering, which is "craving that causes rebirth and is bound up with pleasure and lust and finds delight now here, now there. That is, the craving for sensual pleasures." The third is the "Noble Truth of the Cessation of Suffering" which "is the complete fading away and destruction of this very craving... the liberation from it, leaving no place for it." Thus Buddhism equates desire with suffering, and especially the desire for sensual pleasures. Renouncing one's desire for sensual pleasures is supposedly the path to ending suffering.[265]

Of course, conquered people who feel afraid, nervous, dissatisfied, or miserable are not likely to feel deep pleasure. Foregoing pleasure trains people to accept ongoing dissatisfaction as legitimate and normal.

Deep pleasure is so integral to deep life satisfaction that many healthy nations have encouraged sexual pleasure outside the nuclear family, promoting solidarity and deep friendships. For example, some healthy nations such as the Kulina have special events where men and women can have sex with anyone they want except their spouse, promoting deep connections within and across communities. When sexual pleasure is discouraged, this way of building deep relationships and solidarity is also discouraged.[230]

Religious authorities often put spiritual leaders on a pedestal, as if their spiritual strength was unique or an unattainable ideal. For example, Jesus Christ is often treated as if his grace and spiritual strength was unattainable by mere mortals, and while people should try to learn from him, it's ok and understandable that most people fall far short. This attitude of putting spiritual leaders on a pedestal prevents people from realizing that Jesus Christ's spiritual strength could be normal in a society, and that we should all hold ourselves to that high standard and help each other reach it.[63]

Religion is a major way that rulers have imposed sexism. Authoritarian religions commonly discourage solidarity between men and women by training men to see themselves as superior and training women to submit. The Islamic Quran notes that "Men are the caretakers of women, as men have been provisioned by Allah over women... And righteous women are devoutly obedient..."[270] The Christian Bible says, "I [God] would have you know, that the head of every man is Christ; and the head of the woman is the man."[132] Tibetan Buddhist authorities, prior to the 1951 Chinese takeover, stated that working women were bad luck, and "among ten women you'll find nine devils."[257]

If these holy books really are the Word of an All-Powerful God, then who could argue with them? But what if these religions and "holy" books are simply ideologies imposed on conquered people over many centuries, directly and indirectly training them for obedience?

Tragically, even many non-religious ideologies encourage hurtful attitudes. For example, in my economics class in college, I was taught that humans are basically selfish, and this is good because the "invisible hand of the market" will organize people and channel their selfishness into productive activities that serve capitalist society.

Authoritarian ideologies train people to doubt their instincts, or see obedience as good, or believe they're disconnected from God, evil, shameful, inherently selfish or bad, or only conditionally good (if they obey authority figures). The list of hurtful beliefs is long!

And if people really are so terrible, then of course it's foolish to trust one's neighbors. Thus these beliefs discourage trust too.

Of course, once people have decided to submit, and forgotten what real freedom is like, rulers historically have tricked them into thinking they're free. That's why the USA calls itself "the land of the free and home of the brave,"[29] and Christianity and Islam urge Christians and Muslims around the world to believe they are free even while obeying their authorities.[191,121] Focusing on economic "freedom" instead, the Soviet Union's government claimed it was fostering a revolutionary workers' paradise.[11] And yet these are all merely different dictatorships, where a few people dictate the law and everyone else is expected to obey it.

And what are the results of these hurtful religions and ideologies? Unhealthy nations around the world seem "just how life is" to their inhabitants, including Americans, Iraqis, Koreans, and others.

People learn to accept their obedience as normal. When people demand more jobs, lower taxes, less police brutality, or more funding for schools or hospitals, they're essentially demanding that their authorities please rule them better or more efficiently, and please oppress us a little less. Instead of accepting that they are not free and considering what to do about it, people may believe that they are "losing their rights" or "becoming less free" when their ruling class decides to restrict what speech or actions are allowed.

In unhealthy nations, people only have a single political problem: they are not free. Citizens who ignore this root problem may do all sorts of things that can never lead to deep change, such as voting, having unproductive political arguments with neighbors, worrying about life after death, praying by thinking thoughts in their head, or waiting for a prophet to be reborn and save them. People may do almost anything besides the one thing that could actually improve their spiritual, emotional, and physical lives immensely: *come together in solidarity, create their own laws, and uphold them to create new healthy nations*. This is the path to freedom.

I grew up as a Christian, believing in Jesus and God, and it was difficult for me to accept the perspectives in this chapter. But remember that there is wisdom in every nation and religion. You can keep the wisdom you've found by studying Jesus Christ, Buddha, or Mohammad, and you are free to leave the hurtful or unhelpful aspects of these religions behind.

Many authorities insist that their religion or ideology is "all or nothing" – you either believe everything, or you're cast out as an unbeliever. But that is just bullying, pressuring people to adopt hurtful beliefs or attitudes just to stay in good standing in their community. Each of us has the power and the responsibility to choose which perspectives to embrace and which ones to let go.

Revolutionary Activity #13
Choose what lessons you learn

You have the power to choose which perspectives to learn from others, and which to avoid. Think back to your childhood, and reflect on the beliefs and attitudes you were taught, whether from capitalism, a religion, or anything else. Think of a helpful insight or wisdom that you would like to keep in your life, and think of something hurtful or superficial from that belief system that you do not want to keep.

I grew up as a Christian, and I was taught that Jesus Christ was a good role model. I kept this lesson, and I've learned much about bravery, generosity, and fasting from him. I was also taught that I should be obedient to God and human authorities. But obeying corrupt authorities has never led to justice, so I cultivate integrity and bravery instead of obedience.

Obedient People Act Contrary to Christ's Teachings

There is a common saying that "the winners write the history books." The Roman authorities killed Jesus Christ, and then centuries later they decided which stories would be included in the Holy Bible which they forced on their empire, and they chose which aspects of that Bible would be emphasized in official teachings. And then they pretended that the Bible was the literal word of God, instead of an ideology imposed on conquered people by their rulers to train them for submissive obedience.

Many Christians have grown up since then believing that Christ really was obedient, and obedience really is good and ordained by God. Ruling classes in Europe and around the world have been happy for their conquered people to believe this pro-obedience religious ideology, and they have urged Christian missionaries to spread it, even many centuries after the fall of the Roman Empire.

And tragically, when Christians embrace the pro-obedience Christian ideology instead of really studying Jesus Christ directly, Christians commonly act in ways that Jesus Christ himself would have strongly opposed. Christian missionaries have traveled the world ostensibly to share Jesus' wisdom, but they have urged people to amass wealth and embrace submissive obedience – unlike Jesus Christ, who gave away his things and disobediently stood for justice even at personal risk. They have spread the beliefs that people are inherently sinful, and men have a rightful place over women – unlike Jesus Christ who never taught these things. Wherever obedient Christians have gone, they've spread dictatorships where a few people dictate the laws and the rest submissively obey – unlike their revolutionary spiritual leader Jesus Christ, who opposed the Roman dictatorship he lived in.

As long as people embrace submissive obedience, this sort of deep confusion will remain.

Muslims recognize Jesus Christ as a prophet, and Christians recognize Christ as the only Son of God. I urge everyone to be more like Jesus Christ, and stop being so obedient. *Be like Jesus Christ, and cultivate the spiritual strength to stand for what's right* instead of passively tolerating needless suffering and corruption.

Christians, Muslims, and others endlessly debate when it's appropriate to be obedient, and how authorities can use their power "properly." But healthy nations show the truth: to have a way of life with no corruption, no greed, and no discrimination, where respect is normal, there should be *no unaccountable authorities* and *no submissive obedience.*

This is the root truth behind the *golden rule,* that ancient wisdom which authorities do their best to obscure. Jesus Christ said, "Do to others as you would have them do to you."[192] Buddhist scripture says, "Hurt not others with what pains yourself."[238] A core Islamic Hadith (guidance) says "None of you will believe until you love for your brother what you love for yourself."[180]

When everyone stands for what's right, and everyone expects everyone else in their society to do the same, then the golden rule will be fully realized: each person will treat everyone else as they would want to be treated. The golden rule simply describes the normal way of life in healthy nations.

Fewer people would believe submissive obedience is necessary if they knew what free societies are like where people live without it. Following are some examples showing how whole nations live without *any* submissive obedience.

How Can People Live Together Without Submissive Obedience?

Every nation has laws, whether the nation is healthy or not. But when the laws serve everyone, there's no need for submissive obedience.

In healthy nations, no one forces laws on anybody else that they don't like. *Everyone is expected to uphold their laws, not obey them.* In this way, they have laws they follow, but no obedience. Each person is expected to have the same spiritual strength as Jesus Christ to stand for what's right no matter what.

"Obeying a leader" happens when people do not like the laws or orders they're given, or don't like how the laws are unjustly enforced, but they do what they're told because they would be punished otherwise.

"Following a leader" happens when people like the leader's directions. There is no threat involved. For example, the crowds of people who listened to Jesus *followed* his spiritual leadership without any pressure or coercion because they valued his teachings and service, but they were forced to *obey* Roman authorities whose leadership they didn't like, because they were threatened with punishment for disobeying.

How can a nation have leaders if no one obeys? It's simple: they *choose* the leader whose direction they value, and if that leader disappoints them, they choose a different one. Oren Lyons of the Haudenosaunee said the leaders are "there by the will of the people and when they don't perform, the will of the people will remove them."[182]

Thus people in healthy nations *choose whom to follow, and only follow as long as they value the leader's direction.* This accountability allows them to have strong leaders, but no rulers.

Consider a military setting. In unhealthy nations, each soldier is expected to follow orders of commanders who are not accountable to the soldier, or be severely punished. Soldiers do not choose which commander or which orders to follow.

In comparison, Apache man Geronimo said that warriors would assume various positions of leadership by common consent, and would only keep those positions as long as they led well.[22]

That is, each individual accepted *personal responsibility* to help choose excellent leaders. If a leader disappointed them, they would choose someone else.

In this way, lower-ranked warriors would accept their leader's directions, but they *chose* to accept his directions because they valued his leadership. "Choosing to follow" a leader and "being forced to obey" may superficially look similar to outsiders. But when the warriors knew that the bravest and most selfless warrior among them was their leader, they didn't need to be threatened with punishment because they wanted to follow.

This is normal in healthy-nation militaries: the warriors choose the best leaders and willingly follow them as long as they lead well, but there is zero submissive obedience. This explains why Sioux man Red Cloud said that, before colonization, "We were as free as the winds and like the eagle, heard no man's commands. We fought our enemies and feasted our friends."[111]

Major Ana Maria described the hierarchy in the Zapatista military, and how she needed permission to have sexual partners or get married. The military had strict rules to ensure they maintained cohesion and safety as they prepared and carried out their revolution. And yet, because they chose the best servant-leaders and avoided corruption, even this strict hierarchy and its rules were in service of the greater good, and Ana Maria willingly agreed.[239]

Because each person accepts personal responsibility to *choose who to follow,* healthy nations select incredibly capable military leaders. Healthy-nation militaries were formidable opponents for the United States until the late 1800s, which explains why the US army named so much military equipment after them, including the UH-72 Lakota utility helicopter, AH-64 Apache attack helicopter, and C-12 Huron transport aircraft.[289]

Even children are not raised to submissively obey their parents in healthy nations. People of healthy nations commonly describe life as a spiraling path, where the process of growing from child to elder is the process of taking ever-greater responsibility for oneself and others, continually ensuring the community takes people's and the nonhumans' needs into account.[9,124]

This explains why young people of healthy nations are often very resilient and capable: instead of blindly obeying authority figures and tolerating meaningless or boring schoolwork, they're raised to take responsibility for themselves and others and they're only given meaningful work. Children raised this way are ready for challenges at each stage of life that surprise people in unhealthy nations.[147]

When Jean Liedloff visited the Yequana, she wrote, "I found the complete absence of pressure by persuasion, by the imposition of one individual's will upon another, difficult to believe or understand, despite the Yequana's perseverance in showing me examples of it." Five Yequana men and a 10 year old boy once joined her and other visitors on an expedition far from their village. After a disagreement, the men chose to leave and one called to Anchu, saying, "Come along!" The boy decided to stay with the foreigners far from home, so he responded, "no." The adults just turned and left.[147]

Liedloff wrote, "There was no attempt to force or even to persuade him to come with them." Young Anchu didn't return home to his village for months, but he was always up for adventure, and "never anything but helpful and always happy." When children are raised to take deep responsibility for themselves and others instead of being raised for submissive obedience, they learn their limits, how to take appropriate risks, how to hold good boundaries and honor others' boundaries, and become self-reliant.[147]

Solidarity is a core value in every healthy nation. So what happens when people disagree on something important, such as where to live or whether to fight a war? Don't they still need to choose a leader, and isn't that leader going to make a decision that many of them don't like, and just have to live with?

Actually, no. In healthy nations, when there is a big dispute, communities may split into smaller groups so that each group has full unity. Because they can split up as needed, often there aren't hard feelings and the new smaller communities may remain friends and help each other in emergencies.

For example, Pretty Shield described how her Crow community had a quarrel in about 1832 and divided into two groups, the Mountain Crows and River Crows. Pretty Shield was born a Mountain Crow but went to live with an aunt who was a River Crow. She said, "This separation from my mother and my sisters was in fact not a very real one, because all the Crows came together often." The Crows never considered living unhappily together and letting the majority impose a way of life that the minority resented. After separating, each group had a way of life and leadership that was satisfactory to all, and the groups remained friendly.[149]

Other stories from the Nez Perce[69] and Sioux[68] show that this willingness to split into separate groups while remaining friendly is a common traditional way of respectfully handling major disputes.

When people in gift economies don't worry about private property and land ownership, they have a lot of flexibility when solving disputes. When people in profit economies feel the need to protect themselves and their property from untrustworthy neighbors, it becomes much harder to resolve disputes respectfully.

These stories show that whole nations can live without submissive obedience, where everybody upholds their law but nobody obeys it. When religious authorities train people to think submissive obedience is good and necessary, they're only trying to cement their rule and keep people from seeking real justice and freedom.

Authorities Attack or Kill Our Spiritual Leaders

There is always a tension in unhealthy nations: which leaders will people follow?

Will people follow the laws of their ruling class leaders and lower authorities, with all their corruption and greed? Or will they follow true servant-leaders, the spiritual leaders who seek justice and stand for what's right, even at great personal risk?

Because oppression is normal in every unhealthy nation, spiritual leaders commonly arise to help people take a stand against it. Many spiritual leaders like Jesus Christ and Martin Luther King Jr have helped people in a variety of ways, including sharing resources, trusting their neighbors, releasing shame and increasing self-worth, recognizing false propaganda, and protecting themselves from predatory law enforcement.

Jesus Christ was called a "messiah" or "savior" because the Jews wanted someone to save them. But save them from what? For centuries, Christian authorities have trained Christians to misunderstand Jesus Christ, saying he "died for our sins."[123] Jews certainly wanted a savior, but not because they were sinful – they wanted a revolutionary leader who would save them from oppressive Roman authorities.

Furthermore, Christ did not intentionally die; he chose to do important work knowing that it would cost him his life. He clearly loved his people so much that he helped the hungry[75] and sick[196] even when it was illegal, and he tried to protect them from predatory moneylenders.[74] The Jews wanted a revolutionary leader, and Jesus stood up and did his revolutionary work knowing that authorities would surely kill him for it.[193] And they did.

Martin Luther King Jr likewise confronted deep injustices, working to end racial oppression and imperialism in the United States in the 1950s and 1960s.[139] Like Jesus Christ, he carried on his work fully aware that he would be killed for it.[138] And the United States government did indeed kill Martin Luther King Jr, as extensively documented at a trial in Memphis, Tennessee in 1999.[61]

In unhealthy nations, *authorities consistently attack or kill our greatest spiritual leaders,* the ones who show the most bravery and generosity, who act in deepest service, who work the hardest to end the injustices that always exist when a few people rule over the rest.

Authorities and their police try to maintain order, and what could be more disruptive and threatening of the ruler-based social order than a true servant-leader who helps free their people?

Killing or imprisoning spiritual leaders is a key way that police maintain order. A declassified US FBI memo from the 1960s stated their goal: to 'Prevent the RISE OF A "MESSIAH" who could unify, and electrify, the militant black nationalist movement.' The memo named Martin Luther King Jr as a possible messiah.[103]

Every person is born with intrinsic strength and a moral compass, but many people in unhealthy nations still believe they need authorities' "leadership" and "strength" to keep them safe, unaware that authorities actually attack or kill the wisest, bravest and most generous servant-leaders among us.

This explains how people have been trained to obey corrupt leaders over the centuries. Authorities attack or kill our spiritual leaders and then spread hurtful ideologies or distorted stories to encourage submissive obedience. Authorities also discourage people from learning what free societies are like, where everybody stands for what's right, nobody obeys corrupt leaders, and justice is normal.

It is critically important to choose for yourself what to believe. Ancient spiritual leaders have much to teach, but ancient distortions can keep you from understanding their deepest lessons. As long as you accept submissive obedience as necessary and normal, you will endure endless corruption and greed in your society.

Only by tapping into your own power to choose what to believe and what principles to uphold can you help build a healthy nation without these deep troubles.

Chapter 10: Why Are People So Racist and Hateful?

Many people born and raised in unhealthy nations seem to think that humans are naturally prone to be racist, sexist, and even hateful. Or at least some are.

This is not true. No one is born racist, sexist, or hateful. Every child, regardless of their nation, is born with an open heart, full of curiosity and empathy for others.

However, immersed in unhealthy nations from birth, many babies eventually become confused children who grow up to be racist, sexist, or hateful adults. By then, it all seems quite natural and normal. People are culturally programmed to discriminate against others. That programming is not in our DNA. It has to be taught.

How are racism and other kinds of discrimination taught? It is simple: rulers decide what behaviors and attitudes are ok, and punish people who don't adopt them. People who play along get rewarded, and those who don't get punished, often in confusing ways. Eventually, hurtful attitudes and behaviors become normalized.

A well-known children's story illustrates how authorities impose and maintain racism and hatred, not just in the past, but similar to major events happening in the news today.

Authorities Impose and Maintain Racism and Hatred by Insisting We All Go Along With It

Remember that old story "The Emperor's New Clothes"?

A con man tricks an emperor into believing that he is dressed in beautiful, expensive clothing when, in fact, he is wearing nothing at all. Afraid to be called a fool by this very confident man, the emperor pretends that he really is wearing beautiful clothing, and his close officials go along with it. The emperor then goes out among the public stark naked, and the masses of people pretend to admire his fine clothing. Everybody maintains this pretense until a child blurts out that the emperor is nude.

When I first found this story as a child, it seemed ridiculous. Why would all the adults pretend to believe an obvious falsehood? But I have a question for you – do you think you would point out the emperor's nakedness? Or would you pretend too?

So what does this old children's story have to teach about ignorance, racism, and hatred happening right now?

In this story, the emperor is the ruler, meaning he decides on the laws and how they're enforced, and he can punish people who express beliefs that he doesn't like. The people in this story know that, and they know, consciously or not, that it is safer to go along and believe that he is beautifully dressed, or at least pretend to believe, rather than face the truth. After all, acknowledging the truth could lead to imprisonment or worse.

Over time, this becomes a habit that feels more or less normal for many people living since birth in unhealthy nations.

Unaccountable Authorities Punish Those Who Speak Up

Let's look at some historical examples to see how this works.

In the US pre-Civil War south, chattel slavery was assumed to be good for the slaves by all right-thinking people. Doctors even had a diagnosis called "Draepetomania" where any slave who tried to escape was believed to have a mental illness.[42] Why would they believe such nonsense, even highly trained doctors, instead of simply recognizing the evils of slavery and acknowledging people's healthy desire to escape?

The answer is simple: any white Americans who sympathized with black people and acknowledged the evils of slavery were heavily punished. One man was imprisoned for 10 years for possessing *Uncle Tom's Cabin,* a book that showed chattel slavery in a sympathetic light.[31]

Draepetomania represents a *blind belief* where people believe something because authorities make it the safe or convenient thing to believe, not because it's true. In other words, it was safe for doctors to believe the runaway slaves had mental illnesses, and it was unsafe to see runaways as healthy and slavery as evil.

Likewise in the Soviet Union and China in the mid 20th century, the government and society were assumed to be great and getting better, so any activists who fought corruption were assumed to have mental illnesses too. Many activists were arrested and accused of having mental disturbances and sent to prison hospitals where they were treated like the political prisoners they were. These activists were behaving appropriately and trying to serve their people, and authorities made up theories of mental illness as a cover story to justify imprisoning them.[235]

In this social pattern, authorities punish people for speaking the truth, making it safe and socially acceptable to believe falsehoods. Unfortunately, this can also cause huge amounts of racism and hatred in a society, as authorities encourage people to adopt racist or hateful attitudes, and punish those who don't.

The Ku Klux Klan was a campaign of paramilitary violence operated by wealthy ex-slaveowners in the US South after the US Civil War. Many Americans know that terrible violence was directed at black people to scare them into remaining second class citizens. But few know that this campaign also attacked any white people who sympathized with oppressed black people![228]

Whites who were racist were left alone or even rewarded. Anti-racist white people risked atrocities like rape, murder, and having their house burned. The conservative news media was full of hate for "Dark Savages and white ignoramusses." This has been a major driver of anti-black racism in the US South: authorities promoted that racism to discourage solidarity among poor white and black people. For centuries they brutally punished any white people who stood up to confront racial injustices. Many KKK members were sheriffs and politicians, so the law was part of the problem![211]

Similar stories abound from unhealthy nations around the world. Nazi Germans and Soviet citizens were each trained by their governments to hate the other side during World War II. Anyone who didn't hate enough risked being called a sympathizer and traitor and going to jail. When these authorities wanted war, they propagated hatred among the populace and punished anyone who spoke the truth and refused to hate.[228]

Why did so many Germans learn to hate Jewish people after World War I? The German monarchy, business leaders, and generals had lost the war. Knowing it was a foregone conclusion, they surrendered before the enemy crossed into German territory. Unfortunately, they had lied to the German public, and the media contained propaganda which said they were winning the war until shortly before they surrendered. Thus many Germans were really confused: why did they surrender if they were winning?[228]

The political, military and business leaders wanted to avoid accountability for losing the war and spreading lies, so they propagated a "stab-in-the-back" narrative, blaming Jews, labor activists, liberals, and others for undermining the country.[228]

A tragic number of Germans believed this nonsense, and it wasn't an accident: propagating hate and ignorance towards Jews and activists and blaming them for Germany's WWI defeat was a way for the ruling class to avoid accountability. Tragically this was one step on the road to the Nazis' holocaust a few years later.[228]

People who fall for scams like racism see their neighbors as a threat and argue about nonsense while ignoring the real problems.

And It Continues Today

Racism, hatred, and ignorance can be widely propagated by authorities for many reasons, including to avoid accountability, sabotage solidarity, and promote imperial wars. It can be challenging to recognize because authorities will often punish someone for one secret reason, but publicly accuse them of something different. For example, present-day Germans who oppose war with Russia have been called "Putin-trolls", a reference to Russian president Putin, essentially calling them traitors instead of brave activists trying to stop an unnecessary war.[99]

In another present-day example, the United States currently supports Israel's genocide of the Palestinians and punishes people who publicly oppose it.

Israel has occupied Palestine for decades, keeping Palestinians under intense surveillance. The control was so tight that even many years ago the Israelis were counting the calories of food being allowed in to keep the Palestinians at starvation levels.[60,109]

The Israelis began their all-out genocide in October 2023, with tremendous US support including weapons, ammunition, military intelligence, fuel, and political cover at the United Nations.[49,246] But how bad has the violence really been? Many news stories say that 60,000 Palestinians have died – surely a tragedy, but not genocide.[8]

Before the present conflict started in October 2023, the Palestinian population in Gaza was estimated at 2.2 million.[213] In February 2025, US president Trump stated the Palestinian population was around 1.7-1.8 million.[158] Other estimates confirm this, using normal techniques to estimate military and civilian casualties in war.[122] So between October 2023 and February 2025, Israelis had killed ~400,000-500,000 people through military violence, famine, and disease while extremely few Israelis have died in comparison.[8]

How have the Israeli and American governments trained their populations to tolerate and even support this genocide? You guessed it: spreading racist and hateful propaganda about Palestinians, and punishing anyone who tried to speak the truth and oppose genocide.

Many government statements have called the Palestinians subhumans who deserve immense cruelty. For example, Israel's defense minister Yoav Gallant said, "We are fighting human animals and we are acting accordingly."[245] Israelis have been trained to see Palestinians as a threat on par with Nazi Germany, rather than victims of a cruel occupation.[95]

In Israel, one school girl expressed sympathy with the Palestinians, saying she hoped they could return to their homes soon. She was suspended from school as other students threatened to burn her village down and the Ministry of Education accused her of "incitement against IDF [Israeli] soldiers."[253]

In America, we see similar disturbances. Anyone who tries to acknowledge the truth about Israeli aggression towards Palestinians is accused of antisemitism – as if opposing the Israeli government's genocide and being racist towards Jewish people were the same thing, which obviously they are not.

President Trump is deporting many people for attending what he calls "illegal" protests and he accuses universities of tolerating antisemitism for allowing protests against the genocide.[7] This is only an expansion of the policy under the previous Biden administration, as the genocide clearly has had support from both major political parties the entire time.[300]

Similar manipulative behavior is happening in many unhealthy nations, including Germany[47], Australia[118], France[215], and other European countries[252].

And it's not just the government that tries to scare protesters away from acknowledging the truth: many business leaders want to scare people into submission too. One businessman, Kevin O'Leary, went on television and said that all activists were being monitored with AI-enabled cameras, their protests would be recorded and show up in background checks, and they would never be hired again.[290] In fact, North Carolina outlawed wearing face masks outside to make this surveillance even easier.[200]

Just like American slave owners scared poor and middle class white people into hating black people or remaining silent so they wouldn't oppose slavery, modern day authorities are trying to scare us into submission so we won't oppose their genocide.

And just like authorities have attacked or killed spiritual leaders in the past, the same thing is happening today as authorities attack or kill the activists showing the most bravery, wisdom, and generosity to try to stop the massacre of Palestinians. American authorities imprisoned Mahmoud Khalil for his activist leadership work against the genocide[210], just like the Germans arrested the organizer Majed Abusalama[90] and the British arrested the organizer Huda Ammori.[92] In every country whose rulers strongly support the genocide, thousands of others have also been persecuted for opposing it.

Why are so many governments and corporate leaders supporting this genocide? People can only speculate: is it part of a plan for creating a major new west-Asian trade route through Israel? Accessing gas deposits off the Gaza coast? Developing beachfront real estate? All the above, or something else? When leaders are unaccountable, it can be difficult to know their true motivations.

So let's take stock: the protests are appropriate, the Israeli genocide against Palestine is real, and it's not antisemitic to point these things out. But a strong coalition of American, German, Australian, Israeli, and other business and political leaders around the world have decided to support this genocide, and they're punishing people for standing for what's right by accusing them of antisemitism and using this as a cover story to justify punishing them.

This shows how ancient patterns of nations with rulers or ruling classes are playing out right now. These countries may not have kings, but anytime one person or a group can impose law on the rest, and choose how that law is enforced, we end up with the same kind of tyranny. This is predictable in any society where people are punished for upholding their own law and seeking justice.

Ancient Rome, Germany, the Soviet Union, Israel, Canada, communist China, the capitalist United States – all of them have shown this pattern where unaccountable leaders punish truth-tellers and propagate racism and hatred when it suits them. *All these countries are actually dictatorships: nations where some people dictate the law, and everyone else is expected to obey it.*

This isn't the only dynamic that leads to racism and hate in unhealthy nations. Authorities can encourage divisive racism in many ways. Authorities may encourage one group of poor people to fear and hate another group of poor people, as when poor whites were encouraged to fear and hate poor black enslaved people in the United States in the early 1800s.[228]

Authorities can even generate racism while pretending not to. For example, many governments pretend to administer justice fairly, but actually punish some groups of people with longer prison sentences for the same crime, as seen in academic studies in China, the United States, and the United Kingdom. Then authorities pretend that more-oppressed groups are more inherently violent or bad. Sadly many people fall for these scams of racism and hatred, believing some groups really are better than others.[227]

Authorities impose systemic sexism in similar ways. One investigation by the Organization of American States found that every legal system of every unhealthy nation in North and South America widely discriminates against women in cases of sexual assault and domestic violence.[89] Stories from around the world show that this is common in unhealthy nations, as authorities impose sexism while pretending to treat everyone equally in the so-called "justice" system.[229]

None of this excuses anyone's behavior, but it does explain where troubles like racism, hatred and sexism come from: authorities impose discrimination by treating various groups differently and propagating hurtful attitudes to justify this, rewarding those who go along and punishing those who don't. Sadly, many people follow along to protect their privilege and teach their children to do the same. Eventually, it all seems quite normal. Just the way life is.

When people are trapped with selfish and unaccountable leaders, the results are always tragic. What would it take for a group of people to select the most selfless and honest leaders instead?

Revolutionary Activity #14
Protect yourself from adopting racist or hateful beliefs
When all you hear are terrible stories about a country or ethnicity, it can be hard to remember that they're just people

too. But if you know someone from that group that you admire, you're much less likely to fall for manipulative racist and hateful propaganda.

Think of a country or ethnicity that your government or news media commonly report in very negative ways. Then find a person from there that you can admire or learn from. You could try to meet someone who lives nearby, or if you cannot find anyone, look for stories at the library or online. If you live in the United States, I suggest finding someone from Russia, Iran, or Palestine.

For example, Vasily Arkhipov was a Russian naval officer working on a Soviet submarine during the Cuban Missile Crisis. One day during that tense standoff with the US in 1962, the two most senior officers wanted to launch nuclear weapons, falsely thinking that war had broken out after an American ship dropped explosives near their sub. All 3 top officers had to agree in order to fire the nuclear weapons, but Arkhipov, the most junior of the three officers, did not believe war had broken out, did not bow to pressure, and refused to launch nuclear weapons. He was right, war had not begun, and his integrity under pressure prevented global nuclear war and saved the lives of millions of people.[285]

Finding a person to learn from does not mean you need to support the country's government. But if you're ever tempted to feel racism or hatred towards a whole country or group, the admirable person you find will remind you that they're people too, probably stuck in an unhealthy nation like you.

Healthy Nations Choose Leaders Who Serve the People

Selfish rulers who encourage discrimination and hate contrast vividly with generous servant-leaders of healthy nations. How do healthy nations promote selfless, generous servant-leaders?

They do not just vote every few years and complain about politicians between elections, or pretend that God chose their leaders who are carrying out "His will," despite endless corruption.

It turns out that it is everyone's responsibility to ensure that only the most selfless people become leaders. Can you imagine having leaders who are so humble that they would never campaign for office? How would they even become leaders then?

Martín Prechtel described how Tzutujil Mayan leaders gave away their wealth each time they reached a new level of leadership, putting them on the same level as everyone else – and these leaders were expected to *never campaign for office.*[220]

Likewise, traditional Cheyenne warriors were trained from childhood never to brag about their moments of bravery, instead trusting that other warriors would tell their stories on their behalf.[98]

It's everyone's responsibility to notice people's good deeds and retell their stories so that people's reputation can grow without any campaigning or bragging.

If you want to be able to live in a healthy nation, with leaders who serve the people instead of selfishly serving themselves, *notice other people's good deeds and tell their stories*. This is based on that first core spiritual practice of practical, aware gratitude for the gifts of others. Each good deed is a gift, and one way to receive that gift graciously is to tell the story so that others know.

When you notice someone who consistently tells the truth even when they could get away with lying, tell them that you notice and tell the stories to other people. When someone keeps a promise even when they really don't feel like it, tell the story. When someone consistently shows up to meetings early and well-prepared and helps the group make good decisions, tell those stories. When someone is a source of calm and good humor in difficult moments, or gives generously when they think no one's looking – *tell those stories* so that the person's reputation grows.

This is how a group can select the most humble, generous, honest, and capable leaders, including people who would never campaign for a leadership role. When everyone in a nation practices noticing good deeds and retelling the stories, the reputations of the best leaders grow naturally. When it's time to pick a leader, the people will know who it should be.

Given that some healthy nations have had many tens of thousands of people, and spanned up to 40,000 square miles or more, this practice doesn't just work at the village level, but can help nations of any size choose the best leaders at every level.

I love telling stories of others' good deeds – it's fun! Who doesn't like telling and hearing good news? Who doesn't like encouraging and rewarding good behavior? Every retelling is a little celebration.

One Nootka storyteller described the importance of "the mirror in the eyes of the people you love."[37] When someone feels unseen and unappreciated, it can be discouraging. When people know that their neighbors and coworkers see them and feel grateful for their good deeds, they're likely to do more good deeds in the future. It simply feels good to give to grateful people.

This is the power of that practical, aware gratitude to encourage more good behavior in the world, and every single person has this power. In a healthy nation or healthy community, this is a key way that you can help choose leaders who actually serve the people instead of selfishly serving themselves.

Revolutionary Activity #15
Spread good news to encourage good deeds

You have the power to encourage good deeds and help even the most humble people become leaders. One key way is to notice others' good deeds and retell those stories. Think of a good deed you've witnessed recently, and tell the story so that others know.

Chapter 11: Can Whole Nations Embrace Awareness and Unity?

When I first began doing nature connection practices, I thought I would just connect with nonhumans. It turns out they helped me connect more deeply with people too. If a whole group of people regularly embraced these practices, they could feel closely connected indeed. There would be no place for sexism, racism and hatred.

Every day, I go to my sit-spot and pay attention to the nonhumans. I ask questions like, what plants grow at what times of the year? What birds live there, and how do they interact with each other and the plants? What animals live there or pass through? I learned to pay attention with all my senses. I learned to feel curious about the experiences of the beings around me, and I supplemented my observations with research – both by reading nature guide books and listening to stories from mentors.

Sitting there each day, I wondered, for example, why a bird would constantly look up as they eat. I learned that they stay continuously aware in case predators arrive. I also saw that some species of tree grew near each other, while others did not. Black walnuts, for example, produce a compound which only some plants find toxic, so they grow near sugar maple and box elder but white pines avoid them.

I continually practiced feeling into the experiences of other living beings based on my observations. I imagined being a songbird and how terrifying it would be to have a sharp-shinned hawk swoop out of the sky and snatch me up in an instant. If I were a songbird, I would probably eat carefully too!

Eventually I learned something really cool: plants and animals can help me notice parts of the landscape I can't observe directly. The movement of a bird might indicate a hidden possum moving through low brush. Or, some birds and other animals like deer can see ultraviolet light that is invisible to humans. Many people's clothes reflect ultraviolet light. I might not notice a person hiding in the woods, but some birds can see the ultraviolet light reflected off the clothes. If I notice birds responding to it, I can learn about the hidden person's presence with the birds' help.

The first of the three core spiritual practices – cultivating a practical, aware gratitude – helped me become much more aware of my environment, and grateful for all the life in it.

Over time, I learned to observe more closely, question my assumptions, and empathize with nonhumans, and the same attitudes and skills helped me understand and empathize with other people too. Even people who are not like me.

For example, growing up, I learned that women can get extra sensitive during their period. For years I learned to leave women alone during this time. But as with my nature connection practices, I started asking, "how is this a gift?" or "what does this have to teach me?"

I noticed that some women friends would reject food during their period that they normally ate, and when I asked, they said the food was rancid. I would try it and I couldn't taste any rancidity at first. As I learned to taste my food more and more, I began to notice the occasional rancidity, especially in store-bought food. I realized that the sensitive women had noticed something I couldn't notice. Like the birds, women could show me something about my environment that I could not experience directly. When a woman said some food was rancid, I trusted her even if I couldn't detect it, and I rejected the food too.

And here is the best part: Over time this helped me notice rancidity I couldn't notice before. In other words, listening to others and trusting them helped me grow in ways I could not have grown on my own.

The more I cultivated careful awareness, the more deeply I could see. For example, I'm a white man, and when I hear black Americans repeatedly complain about police brutality, it shows me where my society isn't as fair as it seems in my experience.

When children complain about being forced to sit through boring or meaningless classes at school, they show me that people weren't born to tolerate boredom and meaningless work in adulthood – we have to be trained for it.

As I became more empathetic and observant, I started treating everyone around me like an extension of me, whether men or women or children or nonhumans. Their awareness became an extension of my awareness. I paid attention to what other people observed or how they behaved and let it show me things I couldn't see by myself. I don't blindly trust everyone, but I take care to notice what lessons I can learn from others.

Ultimately, I can only know my own experience, but this doesn't have to limit me when I cultivate deep awareness. With enough practice asking questions and paying attention, I can see others' perspectives even if their experiences are really different from mine. I might not always agree with someone else's point of view, but I can at least understand their perspective which helps me understand their behavior. And when I get it wrong, that just becomes another chance to grow my observation skills and learn.

These nature connection practices are key to generating unity among people and nonhumans in any nation. Once I started really noticing the perspectives of insects, bears and plants, it became easier to notice and understand other people's perspectives.

When everybody embraces these deep awareness practices, mutual understanding and empathy become common, helping any group find and maintain deep unity – even in unhealthy nations.

These practices also help people make fewer foolish assumptions. Assumptions are simply unexamined beliefs. When you continuously pay attention to what you observe, you notice what you know and what you don't know. There's little room for unexamined beliefs.

But this is not the only way that cultivating a practical, aware gratitude can help people maintain unity.

Generating Unity by Giving Thanks Together

The Haudenosaunee show the kind of unity that comes from these nature connection practices. They have a very special Thanksgiving Address where they methodically go through different forms of life and give thanks to each. They thank the medicine herbs for removing sickness and the fish for purifying water. They give thanks to the trees for providing shelter and food. They give thanks to all the divine beings who give so much to create the web of life that we're all part of.[297]

The Haudenosaunee open every gathering with the Thanksgiving Address, calling it the Words Before All Else. While each rendition is unique, the version I learned ends in this way:[297]

Now we have arrived in a very special place where dwells the Great Spirit that moves through all things. As one mind we turn our thoughts to the Creator with Thanksgiving and Greetings.[297]

We have now become like one being, with one body, one heart, one mind. We send our Prayers and special Thanksgiving Greetings to all the unborn Children of all the Future Generations. We send our thoughts to the many different Beings we may have missed during our Thanksgiving. With one mind we send our Thanksgiving and Greetings to all of the Nations of the World.[297]

Now our minds are one.[297]

Healthy nations generate unity in many ways. In this example, I believe the Haudenosaunee become a people of one mind and one heart by collectively recognizing divinity in all things, recognizing their sacred place in divinity, and giving thanks together.

This Thanksgiving Address helps me remember to feel gratitude and feel connected with life. It softens my heart, and it does much more too. It shows how a nation's leaders can encourage unity and awareness rather than division and ignorance.

When I began giving thanks to the nonhumans for their divine gifts, I realized that God is not off in the sky; Creator is alive in Creation. I believe that's what it means to recognize the Great Spirit That Moves Through All Beings, a perspective I've found in many healthy nations. In Christianity, this is called the Holy Spirit. And since Creator is alive in Creation, when people stand in solidarity with the Earth, they're standing in solidarity with Creator.

Being in solidarity with life means being in solidarity with God. Being One with the Earth and being One with God are the same thing. The same three core spiritual practices that generate solidarity among people in healthy nations also generate solidarity between people and all life, and with divinity itself.

Racism and other kinds of discrimination do not have to exist. Whole nations are capable of incredible unity when they base their way of life on the three core spiritual practices.

Revolutionary Activity #16
Cultivate awareness and connection with the living world

No matter how much or little you know, the same basic practices can help you cultivate awareness and connection with the living world. Find a place within 15 minutes of your house where you can observe the wildlife – a place you like to be. Go there every day, practice feeling gratitude for the nonhumans' gifts, and observe what's going on.

What trails do you see? What birds live there, and what are their lives like? Consider what desires and fears each animal or plant has, what relationships they have with each other, and what lessons they have to teach. *I strongly recommend looking for a nature connection mentor or program to help you on your path.*

Revolutionary Activity #17
Seek the truth directly instead of believing rumors

When hurtful and false rumors spread about someone, they can feel very insecure. People want to be seen for who they are, and people want to trust that their friends will actively verify important facts instead of assuming that hurtful, false rumors are true. Next time you hear a hurtful rumor about somebody, cultivate awareness and avoid assumptions by verifying the truth for yourself.

Chapter 12: Selfish Violence vs Selfless Violence

Growing up in the United States, I heard a lot of people say that nonviolence is good, and violence is bad. And sure, peace may be preferable, but when another group attacks, and escape is impossible, a group of people may face a choice: use violence in self-defense, or submit to the attackers.

Even though peace may be preferable, violence isn't inherently good or bad – it's a question of how a person or group uses violence. Do they use violence selfishly, hurting others for their own personal benefit and lying about it? Or do people use violence selflessly in service of the group, in a way that benefits the people and nonhumans they love?

Selfish Violence in Unhealthy Nations

In unhealthy nations where people are not able to hold their leaders accountable, selfish violence is common. Often the leaders want to go to war for selfish reasons that would never motivate the public to go along.

After all, who would want to risk their lives just to help rich people become a little richer? Knowing this, politicians will make up all sorts of fake motivations for the war, and peace activists will notice the lies and try to point out the truth. Then politicians will accuse the peace activists of being traitors spreading enemy propaganda to keep the country from uniting in support of the military. As Nazi German leader Hermann Goering said after World War II, "whether it is a democracy or a fascist dictatorship or a parliament or a communist dictatorship… It works the same way in any country."[93]

Currently in Germany, the United States, and many other countries, anyone who opposes increased war against Russia in Ukraine risks being called a "Putin lover" or "Putin troll" as Vladimir Putin is the president of Russia.[99] Politicians in these countries maintain the fiction that Russia invaded Ukraine unprovoked, ignoring how the NATO military alliance expanded to Russian borders, regime-changed the Ukrainian government in 2014 to put a pro-western-Europe government in power, and armed the Ukrainian military for years for the purpose of going to war with Russia. All these actions were described in advance in strategic plans published by US-funded think tanks. When activists try to avoid an unnecessary war by pointing out these provocations, they are accused of spreading Russian propaganda.[117,171]

A common way for rulers to motivate the public to fight a war that will only benefit the rich is to stage a fraudulent attack, known as a "false flag" attack. Rulers commit violence against their own people, and then blame it on the group or country they want to attack. In 1939, the Soviet military attacked one of their own towns in secret, blamed the Finnish, and used that as an excuse to start the Winter War against Finland.[72] The Nazi Germans burned their own parliament building but blamed it on the communists as an excuse to outlaw the Communist party in Germany.[30]

In 1999, the Russian federal police secretly planted bombs in Russian apartment buildings, and hundreds of people died. Some people became suspicious when a federal parliament member accidentally described one of the bombings before it happened. They became more suspicious when local police actually caught some of the perpetrators planting a live bomb – and the perps turned out to be Russian federal police agents![244]

No Russian authorities were punished for this. But the government blamed the attacks on Osama bin Laden and soon invaded Chechnya on the pretense of protecting Russia from terrorists.[244]

Likewise, the United States government blamed Osama bin Laden for the 9/11 attacks in 2001, and used the attacks as an excuse to invade Afghanistan and Iraq. However, in recent years the US federal police have released documents indicating that a Saudi national on the payroll of the Saudi embassy supported the 9/11 attacks, including helping some 9/11 attackers with lodging, financing, and travel. Other Saudi government agencies offered various kinds of logistical support. The Saudi ambassador was the billionaire prince Bandar, a good friend of US president George HW Bush who was the father of the president at the time of the attacks. Both of their wealth was heavily tied to oil production.[82,83,283,168]

Other evidence casts doubt on official explanations of the 9/11 attacks.[156,81] Somehow, the Saudi royalty and Bush family escaped any investigation of their involvement. Like the Russian government, the American leaders got the war they wanted.

Whether Russia, the USA, Ireland, Germany, France, Tibet, Great Britain, or any other unhealthy nation, the core problem is the same: a few ruling over the many. When rulers or ruling classes exist they always exploit the people in their own society, and this can happen in very disturbing ways.

Many people hesitate to believe these stories, because it is so repugnant to imagine people of one's own country lying and acting so deeply selfishly. It's even more disturbing when it is the unaccountable leaders themselves acting so hurtfully.

This is just a typical problem in nations that tolerate selfishness and abuse, and do not hold their leaders accountable. This sort of selfish behavior continues endlessly, while peace activists are punished for standing for the truth and trying to avoid unnecessary wars.

Stories of Selfless Violence

Stories of collective self-defense show how people can use violence responsibly, in service of their communities and the common good.

Selfless Violence, Example 1: The Black Panthers

The Black Panthers was an American black revolutionary organization active in the 1960s and 1970s. While they had many programs, including making clothing and breakfasts available to poor black children, one of their most famous actions was to have a few warriors trail police cars. When the police officers would pull over another motorist, these Panthers would pull over within seeing distance behind the police car. Without interfering at all, the Panthers displayed weapons, letting the officers know that they would take a stand if the officers acted abusively.[262,177]

These warriors didn't risk violence for personal gain. They acted to protect their community by upholding the laws they lived by and holding the police accountable for misbehavior. They inspired huge numbers of people to join the Panthers because of this willingness to stand for what's right even at personal risk, using violence if needed in service of the community.

Selfless Violence, Example 2: The Apache

The Apache offer another example of selfless violence. Geronimo described how, in 1858, his people believed they were at peace with the Mexicans. When he and many other warriors went into a Mexican town to trade one day, they only left a small force to protect the women, children, and elders. However, when the warriors returned, they found that Mexican soldiers had killed the entire protection force and many of their families. Geronimo had lost more than anyone – his mother, wife, and all his children were dead. He later told his biographer, "I had lost all."[21,23]

The warriors were not prepared to fight the Mexicans that night, so they and their remaining families left to safety. After replenishing supplies, chief Mangus-Colorado called a war council, and the warriors decided to go to war. They invited other Apache groups to participate, and Geronimo went to them one by one, telling them what had happened and asking them to participate in a war against the Mexicans.[21]

There was no draft, and none of the warriors were poor people seeking to escape poverty. Each one decided for themselves to fight as he or she saw fit, knowing the risks and deciding if it was worth it. Geronimo recruited many people.[21]

Finally all the warriors assembled. They set several safe havens where the wives, children and other noncombatants would safely stay, ensuring everyone in their communities was taken care of. Instead of putting the richest or most politically powerful person in charge, the Apache made Geronimo their war leader, knowing he was extremely motivated after what he'd lost.[21]

Finally they tracked down the Mexicans, including two companies of infantry and two of cavalry. Geronimo sent flanking detachments and led advances over hours of vicious fighting. Many Mexicans and Apaches died, but in the end only Apache warriors remained, having vanquished the Mexicans.[21]

The Apache warriors had used violence selflessly to protect their nation, communicating to the Mexicans that they could not attack Apache communities without facing any consequences.

Selfless Violence, Example 3: The Zapatistas

The Zapatistas are a healthy nation in southern North America, many of whose members are from local indigenous nations. After 500 years of oppression by the Spanish and Mexicans and 10 years of careful planning, they rose up in deep revolution on January 1st, 1994. Unlike shallow revolutions that replace one ruling class with another, so that people remain submissive and their lives don't change much, the Zapatistas remembered how to have a healthy nation where everyone upholds their laws.[169]

The Mexican military and the Zapatista military, known as the EZLN, clashed almost immediately in the Zapatistas' home region of Chiapas, Mexico in the south east. Police and military attacked them with dozens of helicopters and many thousands of soldiers.[107]

However, major Ana María said, "the Zapatista Army is very large and is everywhere." They persevered in solidarity with each other and the Earth. Fighting continued until a ceasefire was called after 11 days, and in February an agreement was signed where the Mexican government recognized their autonomy.[241,107]

However, after fighting officially ended, the government promptly began a campaign of illegal paramilitary violence which continued in violation of the agreement. Evidence came out of the Mexican Defense Ministry's "Chiapas 94 Campaign Plan," where they planned to "secretly organize certain sectors of the civilian population" and "train and support the self-defense forces or other paramilitary organizations..."[241]

Neither the Mexican military nor law enforcement stopped the paramilitary fighters from violating all international laws of war. People fired machine guns into Zapatista villages, cut off people's limbs, and many others were disappeared, executed, or displaced from their homes. The leader of the town of Rosario Ibarra had his arm cut off. Women were told their children would be kidnapped if they did not reveal the organizations to which they belonged.[107]

On December 22, 1997, a paramilitary group called Máscara Roja murdered 45 women, men and children suspected of supporting the Zapatistas. Organized crime groups also committed violence, including some with known links to government officials.[241]

Why did the Zapatistas stand up to the Mexican government? Why was it worth going through such difficult times?

Their rallying cry was *Ya Basta!, Enough!* Mexican rulers exploited them "without caring that we are dying of hunger and curable diseases, without caring that we have nothing, absolutely nothing, not a decent roof, no land, no work, no health, no food, no education." Even with elections, they could not choose leaders they respected or avoid corporate exploitation.[84,169]

One commander said, "Para todos, todo, para nosotros nada" – For everyone, everything; for us, nothing. Each person offers their gifts for the good of the group. This person acknowledged that being a Zapatista was difficult. They sometimes only eat hard tortillas, and may fall sick due to poor food. They often sleep on hard floors or can't sleep for days and nights. Their lives are often at risk.[188]

He described their motivation: "As Zapatistas, we have been declared terrorists for simply wanting to live, for asking for food, for health care… For true change, we are ready to die with dignity, in resistance, instead of waiting to die from curable diseases and hunger."[188]

The Zapatistas knew they could create a respectful society if they could just free themselves from Mexican rule. They did not wait until the war was over either. Consider many of the ways they embraced a respectful way of life, right from the beginning.

No one was forced into military service. Each person chose for themselves if they would risk their life in fighting.[106] Women played key roles. Major Ana Maria led the Zapatistas in taking the town of San Cristóbal de las Casas in Chiapas and commander Ramona played a central role in the resulting peace dialog.[239,170] In 2004, 45% of Zapatista army members were women.[178]

They practiced a deep humility, not letting anyone feel like they were special or better than the rest because of their position. When describing their top military leader, Ana María said, "Marcos, like all the members of the [core planning committee], knows nothing and is nothing. Marcos is just another representative..."[107]

Immediately the Zapatistas put into effect laws which they had prepared in advance. Many women had given input to decide the laws they would live by, and after the revolution, sexism dramatically diminished. Interviews with many Zapatista women in 2014 showed that the changes were real and lasting.[170,79,146]

Although they no longer had authorities imposing sexism through the court systems, religion, and other ways, some individuals still had sexist attitudes. They held each other to a high standard so that hurtful attitudes would have no place there.[79]

They passed laws preserving the seas, rivers, and forests. People could keep enough land to sustain their family, but no one was allowed to hoard land or productive equipment. When individuals owned more than a certain number of acres, the extra was redistributed for communal farming.[237]

Redistributing wealth was a crucial part of creating a healthy nation, as it ensured there would be no rich people to try and corrupt the leadership and society from within. When some people are allowed to stay rich, they will inevitably prioritize their own wealth and privilege over the wellbeing of the nation. In other words, they will remain selfish.

By redistributing wealth early on and outlawing hoarding, the Zapatistas essentially removed deep selfishness in their society. This explains why they could have leaders who actually served the people: rich people were not constantly trying to corrupt their leadership because they didn't allow anyone to be rich.

And since redistributing wealth is normal and common in a gift economy, this wasn't just a one-off event. Redistributing wealth is a common, ongoing part of maintaining a way of life based on generous sharing.

The Zapatistas also ended property taxes and vastly reduced rents.[284] Everyone was free to arm themselves, uphold their laws, and organize their own self-protection groups.[144] All prisoners were released except murderers, rapists, and drug trafficking bosses.[119] They developed a system of leadership that ensured that no one passed laws on anyone else. Rather, different layers of councils, each layer covering a larger area, helped coordinate cooperation and collective self-defense as needed.[199]

One fighter said, "We will always carry resistance and rebellion in our hearts, because we are guardians of Mother Earth, we are not the owners… We were born in it, we live in it, we are going to take care of it and we are going to protect it – and if necessary, we will die for it."[241]

The Black Panthers, Apaches, and Zapatistas showed what it's like to use selfless violence in service of the community. No one in these stories used violence selfishly.

I suspect everyone in these stories would have preferred peace. But when the options are either self-defense or submission, each of us must make a choice. They chose selfless violence in service of the people they loved and the Earth. What would you choose?

Revolutionary Activity #18
Judge for yourself when violence is appropriate

Each person can have the strength to judge when violence is appropriate. Think of 3 examples of selfish violence and selfless violence in service of a greater good. If necessary, do research to find three of each. What do the examples of selfish violence have in common? What do the examples of selfless violence have in common? Decide for yourself when you think violence is appropriate, and when it is not.

Revolutionary Activity #19
Learn self-defense

Self-defense is the ultimate act of self-respect. Learn how to defend yourself and the people you love from threats and violent attacks.

Chapter 13: Can Whole Nations Embrace High Standards?

Authorities systematically train conquered people to accept submissive obedience as legitimate and normal. People with this mindset expect little of themselves and others. They don't expect life to be deeply meaningful or others to be reliably trustworthy. Instead, they learn to focus mostly on themselves and pleasing others to protect themselves, rather than standing for what's right. Many people engage in superficial or wishful thinking about social change, and even adopt the ideologies of their abusers.

The consequences of submissive obedience are devastating. Authorities create and maintain all sorts of systemic problems, including widespread corruption, racism, sexism, hatred, child abuse, and greed. Many people accept and then adopt these hurtful attitudes, beliefs and practices as their own, and nearly everyone accepts these problems as inevitable.

Without exception, every unhealthy nation has these intractable problems, and none of them exist in healthy nations living in traditional times.

But our troubles go deeper still.

A person's integrity is their willingness to stand for a culture of mutual respect, including being honest, keeping promises, having an attitude of service, and standing for justice. But integrity becomes rare when people are forbidden from standing for justice and solidarity is sabotaged. Instead, low integrity, cowardice, superficiality, ignorance, and low self-worth become common.

When people accept that corruption and greed are unavoidable aspects of their nation, they also come to think that these unwelcome personal qualities like cowardice and superficiality, while tragic, are unavoidable too. When these qualities start to seem normal, people's expectations or standards for themselves and others fall. After all, why expect deep integrity or generosity from anybody if you're just going to be let down?

But there is good news. It is possible to live without troubles like discrimination and corruption. It's also possible to live in a nation where everyone embraces integrity, bravery, and generosity so that neighbors can deeply trust each other. Many stories of healthy nations living in traditional times show how high our standards can be, and reveal how low our standards currently are.

The path to creating new healthy nations requires learning how to hold ourselves and others to high standards so that integrity, generosity, and other attractive qualities become common.

Healthy Nations Show How High Our Standards Can Be

Integrity: Every legal system requires testifying under oath and threatens people with severe punishment for lying. The assumption is that people can't be trusted unless they fear punishment.

In contrast, integrity was so pervasive among the traditional Apache that no one was compelled to take an oath because, according to Geronimo, "it is not believed that they will give false testimony in a matter relating to their own people."[24]

Physical resilience: Crow woman Pretty Shield described how physically resilient her people used to be: "[W]hen I was young, if in winter a person fell into icy water, he got out, took off his wet clothes, and rolled in the snow, rubbing his body with it, and got warm. Then, after squeezing out the water, he put on his clothes and forgot about getting wet... Now my people wear gloves, and too many clothes. We are soft as mud."[151]

Generosity: A Christian missionary visited the Ojibway, Cheyenne, Cree and Sioux nations, describing how Jesus Christ gave away all his possessions, urged others to do the same, and dedicated his life to feeding, healing, and protecting his people. The missionary was told that, prior to colonization, Jesus Christ's level of selfless generosity was normal among them.[63]

Meaningful Education for Young People: One Nootka storyteller described how the women would often have their moon time at the same time each month, and they would go to a special house and enjoy a four-day party. They would sit on special soft moss and give their blood back to the Earth and play games and talk. Women would massage each other and make special tea for cramps. This became a big opportunity for older women to mentor younger women. For example, young women learned the special Frog posture that could help relieve cramps and make childbirth easier.

Benefitting the Earth: Stories abound of people of healthy nations benefitting or enriching the Earth as a normal way of life. Robin Kimmerer described how Black Ash trees became more abundant in regions where it was respectfully harvested by Mohawk and Potawatomi basket makers, and this remains true today.[131] Apache man Stalking Wolf described how he respectfully harvested a sapling to make a powerful bow so that the forest also benefitted.[33]

These are high standards. Total integrity is normal, and Jesus Christ's level of selfless generosity is considered normal too. Physical resilience and meaningful childhood education are also baseline expectations. Their normal way of life benefits the Earth around them, increasing the natural abundance that they depend on.

When people bring out the best in each other and hold each other to high standards, whole nations can maintain a baseline of mutual respect among the people, and between people and the Earth.

Remember, members of nations such as the Potawatomi, Crow, Apache, and Nootka are people like anyone else. They have attitudes, skills and awareness that anyone could cultivate – including you and other strong and caring people you know.

Revolutionary Activity #20
Hold yourself and others to a high standard

Think of a time when someone had faith in you, maybe even more faith than you had in yourself. Did someone help you find the self-respect to leave an abusive relationship? Did a coach help you cultivate the discipline to train at your sport and be the best you could be? Did a teacher help you realize you could be great at whatever you put your mind to? If this mentor did their job properly, they did not shame or punish you, but helped you see your unmet potential and urged you to reach it – to be your best self, and not settle for less. Think of a time when someone brought out the best in you, holding you to a high standard.

Watch for an instance where someone lets themselves or others down. Perhaps they lie to someone or to themselves, give up on a goal too easily, or tolerate an unsatisfying relationship or job without trying to change it. Help them find the strength to do what they need to do.

Revolutionary Activity #21
Make it easy for others to hold you to a high standard

Often, when one person feels upset by another, they'll struggle to speak clearly and respectfully. Whenever someone expresses frustration with you, or offers you constructive feedback, actively look for the lesson so that you can grow from the experience. Repeat the lesson back to them to ensure both of you agree on it. Make it easy rather than difficult for others to give you constructive feedback and hold you to a high standard.

Seeing the Trap of Low Standards

When people accept submissive obedience as normal, many unnecessary problems arise. These problems may seem inevitable, just part of the human experience. But in truth, they're only problems in unhealthy nations where people are trained not to hold themselves or each other to high standards.

Low Standards for Children

How adults treat kids and young adults offers many examples of low standards and the terrible problems that result. People in unhealthy nations often assume that it's normal and inevitable for teenagers to act rebelliously, or that teenage years have to be awkward and stressful. However, children in healthy nations are expected to take ever greater responsibility for themselves as they grow, becoming self-reliant by their teenage years or even contributing to their families.

When children are not raised from birth to follow this natural process toward maturity, they face a dilemma in their teenage years. Biologically, teens have a natural urge for independence, but most haven't been prepared for it by this age. Instead, the vast majority suffer through endless boring classes which prepare them for unfulfilling jobs later in life.

Healthy nations show how capable and confident children and young adults can be, and how teenage awkwardness and rebelliousness are merely symptoms of living in unhealthy nations.

Martín Prechtel describes how, among the Tzutujil Maya, both boys and girls were sufficiently mature and skilled to contribute to the family by the age of 12, carrying their own weight or more.[222]

Young Nootka boys and girls were trained to have very strong physical endurance and very high standards. One Nootka woman storyteller said, "every day we had to get our bodies ready. So that when the time came to go from bein' a girl to bein' a woman, we'd be ready." Girls learned many skills including gathering fiber and weaving. When puberty arrived, the young woman would have a rite of passage where, after a big party with her family and friends, she dressed up in her finest clothes and was taken out into the ocean. Far from shore, she would strip down naked and dive into the ocean and the boat would leave her all alone. She would swim back to her family and friends who lit a fire on the beach for her return. As she approached, "they'd start to sing a victory song about how a girl went for a swim and a woman came home." Children raised with meaningful mentorship every day were ready for adulthood and other adults recognized it. When teenagers are treated respectfully, there is nothing to rebel against![34]

Many adults assume that young teenagers cannot be mature enough to have respectful sexual relationships, but this is only typically true in unhealthy nations. When children are raised to take responsibility for themselves and others, feel their feelings, understand risk, and have good boundaries, the Mosuo show that young adults can have respectful and joyful relationships as teenagers.[243]

When a Mosuo girl reaches puberty, her new bedroom has two doors, one for the family to enter and one all her own so she can easily have lovers visit. One visitor described the young women as "sassy and confident," and noted the lack of "broken homes," impoverished single mothers, and shameful divorces.[243]

In unhealthy nations, a major obstacle to having many sexual relationships is the fear of pregnancy and becoming a parent before the person is ready. However, expecting the two sexual partners to be the sole parental figures for any child is unnecessarily limiting. Each Mosuo man knows from boyhood that he will be a parent figure for his sister's children, and this frees both men and women to have sex without worrying about which man fathered which child. Mosuo women know they will always have a family and parenting support regardless what happens with their sexual relationships, which takes a lot of pressure off of them. One Mosuo woman described how they share parental responsibilities: "In place of one father, Mosuo children have many uncles who take care of them... We also have many mothers, because we call our aunts... 'little mother.'" Others outside the family help too.[243]

This way of arranging parenting responsibilities allows both men and women to have sexual partners without worrying about who the biological father is, making it easier for both men and women to have more sex while ensuring children are well cared for. They created a way of life where men, women and children get their needs met without unnecessary sexual restrictions, and this helped young adults feel secure.[243]

Jean Liedloff acted as a physician among the Yequana, and she noted, "All [their] behaviour contradicted the assumptions I held about how children behave." A four-year-old came to her all alone with a gaping wound and kept his composure through the pain, and a 9-year-old came with an abdominal wound. There was no needless worry, and they didn't need sympathy. Even the 9-year-old's mother showed no anxiety. After all, everything that could be done to address the injury was being done. The boys recovered.[147]

Liedloff ascribed these children's emotional resilience and self-confidence to having sufficient time in their mother's arms in early childhood, being raised with healthy boundaries, and being corrected without guilt or shame after any mistake.[147]

She watched how, if a young child sullied the floor in the family's house, he would be told sternly to go outside and not to make a mess inside. Thus the adults set healthy boundaries, but "he is not told that he is bad or that he is always doing the wrong thing. He never feels he is bad, only, at most, that he is a loved child doing an undesirable act." Adults trusted that the children were good people who made a mistake, not bad people who needed to be shamed into obeying. Shame, insecurity, and emotional fragility were absent among the Yequana, including among children and teenagers.[147]

In unhealthy nations, troubles at the national level are reflected in many families. Adults who aren't allowed to take deep responsibility for their community or nation – because they're not allowed to choose their laws or uphold them – often struggle to raise children to take full responsibility for themselves and others. Adults who are not allowed to hold others, and especially their leaders, to high standards of good behavior struggle to respectfully hold children to high standards. Parents who are used to submissive obedience often expect the same from their children, or they may reject rules entirely and not hold firm respectful boundaries, tolerating careless or disrespectful behavior. None of these attitudes teach children how to have good boundaries or high standards.

Revolutionary Activity #22
Hold firm boundaries without encouraging shame or guilt

Next time someone acts hurtfully towards you or someone you care about, acknowledge the problematic behavior, the impact it had, and what behavior you would rather see. Do not put the other person down or make any hurtful or dismissive comments to them. Trust that they want to know if they made a mistake and will grow from the experience. Many people are not used to being treated this way, with both respect and healthy boundaries, so be ready to help them understand what you expect of them. If they truly are not willing to hold themselves to a high standard, you will see this clearly, and you can decide not to cooperate any more.

Revolutionary Activity #23
Notice how you tolerate boredom

Tolerating boredom is a key way many people learn to live with low standards. Anytime you feel bored, notice how you distract yourself. Do you seek fake excitement or connection by watching TV, playing video games, gambling, watching pornography, counting your money, or having meaningless arguments? Do you stay busy with work, or ignore your feelings with alcohol or drugs? One major source of boredom is feeling isolated and mostly thinking about oneself instead of how to help others. Next time you're bored, do something helpful for a friend, family member or neighbor so that they feel grateful to you. Ask the other person for suggestions if necessary.

Low Standards for Politics

Low standards are pervasive in politics.

Politicians may brag about being "tough on crime," but they never talk about *ending crime*. Ending crime would require people to create a healthy nation like the Mosuo, who have so little crime that their language has no words for "murder" or "rape."[243]

Many citizens in democracies care deeply about their society but knowingly vote for evil candidates anyway as "the lesser evil." How can people think they're free if they can only choose between more or less evil political leaders? At its root, "evil" means "corrupt" or "selfish," describing someone who prioritizes their own needs at the expense of the group.

Even so-called liberation movements will be disappointing as long as people accept their submissive obedience as legitimate.

For example, black people and women were both treated abominably in the United States at the start of the 1900s, facing severe discrimination in the workplace, courtroom, and other areas of life. After more than a century of "women's liberation" and "black liberation" movements that focus on "civil rights," what is the result? Women and black people can now become corrupt politicians, just like they can be selfish rich business owners, corrupt judges and police officers, and well-paid wage slaves.

Women and black people have essentially been offered a smaller serving of the same bad deal that white men have had since the United States' founding: if you're willing to embrace selfishness and sacrifice your integrity, you too can have a comfortable position in your corrupt society, and even a small chance at getting rich. Plenty of women and black people have taken this deal, just like many white men have taken it for centuries. In practice, these were movements not to seek liberation, but to increase people's privilege and reduce the abuse they faced.

Since the United States remains an unhealthy nation, and *every* unhealthy nation *always* has racism and sexism, these troubles persist today. When people accept submissive obedience as normal, they will even have low standards for liberation movements.

Instead of seeking real freedom, authorities trick people into thinking that "freedom" means being able to do whatever you want, so the way to become free is to get rich. But this is faux-freedom, the ability to act selfishly without restraint. No matter how rich you get, you still won't be allowed to stand for justice. You'll just have a more comfortable place in an abusive society.

Real freedom comes when everyone in a nation stands for what's right as a normal way of life, so everyone enjoys justice, shared resources, protection, and respect among their neighbors.

I certainly do *not* suggest anyone quit their job. However, "climbing the ladder" to get better-paying jobs is not the path to freedom. The further up the ladder you climb, the further you are from *the most secure feeling in the world* – the priceless security that comes from living in a supportive, respectful, generous community that you trust has your back.

Revolutionaries like the Black Panthers and Zapatistas often kept working their jobs as they sought to free their people. Black Panther Don Cox put it well: "use what you got to get what you need."[51] Making money shouldn't be the end-goal. Just like the Tzutujil Mayans and Huron who liked to get rich so they could give it all away, make money so you can do the most good in service of the people and nonhumans you love.

Low Standards for Women

Unhealthy nations consistently train people to idolize the rich and powerful, and this has caused many women to have low standards for women leaders. Many parents encourage their daughters to pretend to be a princess and fantasize about being royalty, even though kings and queens consistently exploit the people they rule.

Many young women aspire to leadership positions in politics, but corrupt women politicians are no better than corrupt men. British prime minister Margaret Thatcher oppressed labor unions,[145] and

American secretary of state Hillary Clinton approved extra weapons sales to countries that bribed her, even while State Department reports described those countries' many human rights abuses.[247]

Selfish women business executives can likewise do just as much harm as selfish men, leading corporations that produce vast amounts of toxic chemicals[236] or lobby for needless wars while supplying the weapons.[15,152]

A common theme in healthy nations is *balance,* ensuring both women and men have influence without corruption. Male and female partners usually served as Tzutujil Mayan chiefs together.[218]

The traditional Cherokee had a White Council of women who led during peacetime and a Red Council of men who led in war. Cherokee woman Rebecca Adamson said, "The goal was the balance, the harmony, the bringing together of both wisdoms and both energies for the good of the Nation."[186]

In the Haudenosaunee Confederacy, a clan mother selects a male leadership candidate who goes through several stages of approval. Her entire clan must support him, then the council of leaders must approve, and finally anyone in the Confederacy may veto if he or she has doubts. If the candidate does not pass any stage, the clan mother finds someone else, ensuring that every leadership candidate has the support of a trusted elder woman.[182]

There are many ways for wise and capable women to serve their people. But neither men nor women politicians will address the deepest injustices as long as the nation has low standards.

Low Standards for Men

Masculine mentors in healthy nations consistently emphasize two qualities: integrity and bravery. These are qualities for everyone to embrace, and they are repeated often when men train boys.

Nez Perce chief Joseph's advice to an American boy was simple: "be brave and tell the truth."[294] Wikis' Cheyenne uncle likewise taught him there was "one thing more important than anything else, and that is to be brave... If you do that, the people will all know of it, and will look on you as a man." He also said, "always be truthful and honest with all your people."[96]

Men of healthy nations show what it's like to live with total integrity and bravery, and they reveal just how far from this high standard most men in unhealthy nations typically live.

Apache man Geronimo described how young men were expected to show "no color of cowardice, or weakness of any kind." All boys were trained to be warriors who would protect their people. Geronimo stated the minimal, entry-level requirement: "[once the youth] has proven beyond question that he can bear hardships without complaint, and that he is a stranger to fear, he is admitted to the council of the warriors in the lowest rank."[22] Only young men with this depth of bravery were considered ready for marriage.[23]

Huron men intentionally practiced bravery throughout their adult lives so they would be ready to protect their people from any injustice or threat. This included intentionally causing themselves pain to practice maintaining composure under duress.[278]

Jean Liedloff was impressed by the strong, positive male presence she witnessed in Yequana households which she described as relaxed, peaceful and serene. The men were not permissive, holding everyone to the highest standards, and boys loved to measure themselves against their fathers. Everyone took "pride in doing their best, in living up to the men's expectations as well as to one another's... By his behaviour, his own dignity and excellence in what he does, he shows their society's ways to the young."[147]

Sioux man Ohiyesa described how he was trained not to care for money or possessions, "because a true Indian always shares whatever he may possess." He said, "We never [had] any money... we valued nothing except honor." Sioux men would bravely share their last food with a hungry neighbor.[66]

Women often ask *where are all the good men?* In feminist literature around the world, this is a common question going back to the dawn of unhealthy nations.[234]

I did not know what a good man was until I studied healthy nations where boys are raised to consistently practice integrity and bravery, becoming good men willing to confront any injustice or threat to their people.

Stories from healthy nations show what it's like when women can trust all the men. One Cheyenne boy named Wikis was 5 or 6 years old when his village was suddenly attacked, and men instantly ran towards the threat while women gathered the children. Wikis said, "My mother rushed out and caught me by the hand… and then she stopped and in a shrill, sweet voice began to sing; and other women that were running about stopped too, and began to sing songs to encourage their husbands and brothers and sons to fight bravely; for enemies were attacking the camp…"[97] The women would not have sung for untrustworthy men.

All these stories show how low our standards for men are. When boys are trained for submissive obedience, they are trained for cowardice instead of bravery and humiliation instead of dignity. This upbringing trains boys to "hold back" or "shut down" core parts of themselves, becoming spiritually lost as they do not know how to relate to themselves and the world in a good way.

Boys are raised to ignore their humiliation and cowardice so it seems normal. Some grow up to be people-pleasers who stand for nothing, just keeping life easy. Others become selfish, standing only for themselves. That Martin Luther King Jr and Jesus Christ are so revered shows how rare profoundly good men are in unhealthy nations.

Spiritually lost men may preen on social media, flaunt their wealth, or spend vast hours playing video games. Some men live vicariously by watching movies or professional sports, or they focus on superficial hobbies or making money, or obsess over political and religious dogmas.

In 1877, the American military captured some Cheyenne women and children. The very next day, 500 Lakota and Cheyenne warriors launched an attack to try to retrieve them.[181] Women and children suffer many sexual and physical assaults in unhealthy nations – where are the good men who would band together to stop this?

Men who have been systematically trained to deny their feelings and not to follow their sacred path may abandon their family or beat them, or get lost in drugs or alcohol. Even among men who avoid these troubles, how many boys feel grateful to their fathers for holding them to high standards? How many girls feel grateful to their fathers for showing them what a good man is like? Too few!

Some men join the police or military where they pretend to serve the public while obediently taking orders from unaccountable leaders, so they actually protect the rich and powerful. Authorities consistently threaten the careers and even lives of brave police whistleblowers who call out the police's own illegal activity, scaring the remaining officers into submissive obedience.[231]

Behind this superficiality, many men struggle with nagging questions like "when does life become meaningful?" or "why am I even here?" As Henry David Thoreau put it, "The mass of men lead lives of quiet desperation."[272] This also explains the saying that "Every man dies. Not every man really lives."[91]

Living a life of submissive obedience is not satisfying. Tolerating injustice and meaningless work is not satisfying. Debating politics while pretending that the whole system isn't corrupt is not satisfying. Living with low standards is not satisfying.

Men have a deep urge towards freedom, but few know what freedom even means because they have been systematically misled and poorly trained from birth. Unhealthy nations don't raise boys to be good men because good men would protect their people from oppression and lead them to freedom, and this is forbidden.

To male readers, I say this: It is time to raise our standards. Cultivate your integrity and bravery, and make friends with others who also hold themselves to a high bar. There's a reason healthy nations train men to prefer a brave death to a humiliating long life. Tolerating humiliation leads to all the troubles of abusive nations. You would live longer but feel half dead inside.

Of course, in unhealthy nations some amount of submissiveness is required in order to survive. The Deepest Revolution requires the bravery and integrity to strategically choose when to submit and when to take a stand to do the most good. When you value and cultivate these qualities with others who hold each other to high standards, you will grow a depth of spiritual strength that few men in unhealthy nations ever achieve.

The path for a group to build a new healthy nation and live in freedom will require everyone to hold themselves and others to high standards. To do this, we must learn how to spiritually grow without feeling guilt or shame.

To Have High Standards, Learn to Grow Without Guilt or Shame

Feelings of shame and guilt are some of the biggest obstacles to spiritual growth. They can also make a person resistant to receiving feedback from others, making it difficult for people to hold each other to high standards of behavior. People may resist feedback because they have been taught to feel shameful and guilty in the past, or treated unfairly, and don't want this to happen again. Others may have subconscious shame or guilt from childhood that gets triggered, creating automatic insecurity and defensiveness.

Therefore, to effectively hold yourself and others to high standards and help people grow from their mistakes, learn how to pursue personal and collective growth without shame or guilt.

A key requirement is to have the attitude that, when someone lets you down, they are a *good person making a mistake,* not a bad person being bad. Trust that they want to show up in a good way and just don't know how. There's something they're missing, but if they could see it, they would learn and show up better.

Some people are so stuck that they don't grow even with repeated respectful feedback, and you may need to set boundaries and not allow their hurtful behavior in your life or community anymore. But if someone acts hurtfully and you start with the attitude that they're "bad," they will be resistant to any feedback that you offer.

Revolutionary Activity #24
Learn without guilt or shame

Think of a time you made a mistake and you felt guilty or shameful in response, perhaps because an adult urged you to feel this way. How much harder did those feelings make it to learn from your mistake? How helpful would it have been if the person trusted that you wanted to learn from the experience? Next time you make a mistake, learn what you can, notice any feelings of guilt or shame, and just let them go.

Everything is a Skill That Can be Practiced Without Guilt or Shame

Think of a skill you learned as a child. Imagine, for example, that you learned to ride a bike, including smaller skills such as steering or peddling. To get better at steering, what did you do?

You practiced: you tried your best to ride straight, and sometimes you went straight and sometimes you didn't. When you made a mistake, you figured out what to learn and then practiced more. The more you practiced, the more proper technique became normal.

Integrity, awareness, gratitude, and generosity are also skills, and you can practice them intentionally too. Practice approaching life with these qualities, and notice when you fall short. Practice being aware of yourself whenever you make a mistake, such as ignoring certain feelings or being afraid to tell the truth and lying instead.

It is ok to feel disappointed if you fall short. But if you feel insecure or like you are inherently bad or not good enough, this is unhelpful shame. If this feeling arises, acknowledge it and let it go. Just recognize that you made a mistake, learn from it, and do better next time. If you disappointed someone else, acknowledge your mistake, do your best to make it right, learn any lessons you can, and commit to doing better. You are just practicing and learning.

And just like you practiced steering before going for a long bike ride, you can practice these beautiful qualities outside the normal flow of life. For example, bravery is the ability to remain conscious and do what you know is right even if you feel uncomfortable or afraid. To practice, put yourself in uncomfortable or scary situations and practice maintaining your composure. If you're scared of dancing, face your fear and go dancing. If cold water feels uncomfortable, practice keeping your composure in cold water. Learn to feel *comfortable in the midst of discomfort* so that nothing causes you to ever "hold back" or "shut down" parts of yourself.

The book *One Disease One Cure* contains many more suggestions for cultivating bravery, integrity, and other qualities.

Spiritual growth can be joyful when you approach it without shame or guilt, with friends that bring out the best in each other. Mistakes really are just learning opportunities. These attitudes allow you to take accountability for your mistakes and grow without shame.

For me, "spirituality" means how you relate to yourself and the world. Thus, "spiritual growth" means learning to relate to yourself and the world in a better way, including with integrity, awareness, bravery, joy, generosity, respect for the Earth, and healthy personal boundaries. The three core spiritual practices lead to spiritual growth by helping you relate to the world with gratitude, by identifying and giving your sacred gifts, and living in reciprocity.

Recognizing two complementary truths will accelerate your spiritual growth. First, *you are already perfect,* even with all your faults. Second, *you have unmet potential,* and you must strive to fulfill it to give your deepest love. The first truth is about self-acceptance, and the second is about growth.

Self-acceptance is the foundation for spiritual growth, so your growth will be limited without it. If you feel self-doubt or low self-worth, focus on total self-acceptance. You are perfect as you are now, faults and all, and you're basically ok. With this self-acceptance, see your unmet potential, and grow to meet it.

When you hold yourself to high standards, your rate of growth will increase. You won't waste time feeling shame and guilt. You will just notice your mistakes, learn from them, and move on.

These shame-free and guilt-free attitudes to spiritual growth are essential. Embrace them to hold yourself and others to high standards and create relationships of deep trust, where qualities like integrity, bravery, awareness, and generosity are normal.

Revolutionary Activity #25
Practice bravery

Consistently facing your fears is one key way to cultivate bravery. Think of a fear that you're avoiding right now. You may have lied and you're afraid to admit it, or you're afraid to quit an unsatisfying job. Face your fear, recognize that you can handle whatever comes, and do what you need to do.

Chapter 14: This Pervasive Abuse Must End

Sioux man Sitting Bull said, "The life of white men is slavery. They are prisoners in their towns or farms." How do you feel reading that? When I first read this, I thought he must be exaggerating.[142]

How can well-off, even middle- or upper-class people be prisoners?

Just as prisoners have no influence over how the prison rules are enforced, the vast majority of people in unhealthy nations have no influence over how the laws are created or enforced. And just as prisoners have little influence on what happens in the cell across the hall, the vast majority of citizens, when they behave obediently, have little influence over what happens around them. When huge numbers of people resign themselves to tolerating abusive behavior instead of seeking justice, then abuse becomes the norm.

Sadly, child sexual abuse runs rampant in these conditions, including by unaccountable religious, business and political authorities. For example, researchers in Germany, Ireland, the USA and Australia have found many thousands of child sexual abuse victims just from Catholic priests in each country. One investigation into Catholic abuses in France alone found over 216,000 child sexual assault victims between 1950-2020. Universally, higher Catholic Church authorities covered up or stalled investigations into the abusive priests.[266]

Child rape can become quite normalized. One boy was raped by monks in Buddhist Tibet and complained to other monks. He said, "they shrugged and said simply that that was just the way things were."[281]

Many secular authority figures have also raped children, and few have faced any accountability at all – clearly too few to deter any others. Famous British media personality Jimmy Savile sexually assaulted dozens of underaged people as young as 8 years old from the 1960s-1980s. When a young woman complained to British Broadcasting Corporation (BBC) staff about his inappropriate behavior, the staff evicted her from the premises. Another young woman was told, "keep your mouth shut, he's a VIP."[250,251]

An orphanage in Portugal was revealed to house a huge child sexual abuse operation in 2002, although the police and the Portuguese president were notified of the abuses by several boys and even a government minister in 1980. Several low-ranking men were prosecuted, but none of the wealthy international clients who flew in to spend time with the boys faced justice. Of course, the police and politicians who "failed" to investigate likewise went unpunished.[275,274]

How do you think the Portuguese people felt watching these televised legal proceedings carefully ignore the worst perpetrators? They clearly did not prosecute the most powerful politicians, police, and businessmen who were involved – how would you feel knowing all those people still had their wealth and power?

Tragically, such disturbing troubles are common in unhealthy nations that punish you for seeking justice. Thus similar stories can be found in the United States.

In the late 1980s in Omaha, Nebraska, a child sexual abuse operation was discovered based in the child foster care system. Investigators found child sexual abuse victims who described many satanic rituals and named many powerful people as abusers, including judges, politicians, and wealthy business executives. National figures were involved too, including billionaire George HW Bush, who at various times was a US president, vice president, and CIA director. Fifteen knowledgeable people died violent deaths during the investigation, and none of the perpetrators faced justice.[55,56]

Nothing occurred in any of these cases to suggest that the institutionalized child sexual abuse ever ended. People in all these unhealthy nations go on about their lives as if this rampant child abuse isn't still happening all around them.

How much child abuse is happening all around you right now, from authorities or other abusive adults? Do you know? If you found out, and if you decided to personally take action to stop the abuse, what would happen? That's right – you would be punished, because only the police are allowed to actively enforce the law. You would be punished for seeking justice and upholding the laws you live by.

You would be punished if you intervened to stop child abuse, just like you'd be punished for trying to free unjustly imprisoned people or trying to stop a genocide.

Just like all of your neighbors, you would be punished for standing for what's right, and because so many people accept this way of life as legitimate, abusive behavior is widespread, with the worst predators having the most wealth and power.

A staggering level of abusive behavior always occurs when people allow themselves to be ruled and choose not to stand for what's right. All these disturbing troubles will continue until you and the people around you can generate a healthy nation, where everyone stands for a culture of mutual respect, and nobody rules over anybody else.

Healthy Nations Don't Abuse Children

Can you imagine a world without child sexual abuse? Not just a world with more self-defense classes, or stronger laws, or better ways of supporting victims, but a world without *any* child sexual abuse?

This world is possible. Healthy nations in traditional times do not have child sexual abuse. When the Nootka first encountered Spanish conquistadors, they did not encounter any women. Instead, the Spanish "only brought men and young boys who got used as women whether they liked it or not."[39] Even in their first interaction with Europeans centuries ago, the Nootka noticed regular child rape that remains so common in unhealthy nations to this day. After a period of uneasy interactions, the Spaniards kidnapped, raped, and murdered two Nootka girls.[40]

The Nootkas' response shows that they had never experienced child sexual assault until encountering an unhealthy nation:

"...The people had no way of understandin' what had happened. There'd never been anythin' like this in all the time since the beginning of life, and so they could only stare at the proof of horror and feel numb shock. They could see what had been done, but they couldn't understand how, or why. It had been hard enough to believe the Keestadores [conquistadors] would force a grown

woman to have sex when they didn't want, but the thought of sex with a child was just too horrible for the people to even imagine, so they didn't know what to think.[40]

The old woman examined both the babies, and it was as if the sure evidence of what she found shook the centrepost of all creation, and threatened the here and now as well as the past and future..."[40]

The Nootka lived without child sexual assault until they encountered an unhealthy nation. This shows that it is possible for a whole nation to have *zero* child sexual assault.

I knew child rape was vile, but why was it so bad that it would "[shake] the centrepost of all creation" and "[threaten] the here and now as well as the past and future?"[40]

Healthy nations see any disrespect as a cultural wound that affects everybody, and the Nootka recognized that this child rape was a severe disrespect and therefore a severe cultural wound. If this disrespect wasn't fully addressed, everything was at risk, and nothing would be safe.

The Nootka soon allied with neighboring groups and successfully killed all of these conquistadors. They saw how important it was to their nation's survival to protect themselves from predators.[41]

This shows the importance of maintaining that internal baseline of mutual respect. As the stories of widespread child abuse in unhealthy nations show, once a nation allows disrespect and tolerates predators, abusive behavior becomes normalized.

What Is It Like to be Conquered? And What Does That Have to Do With You?

Living in an unhealthy nation means being trapped with predators. The vast majority of people accept this as normal and inevitable, even if tragic. Living with predators is "just the way life is."

But all of us have ancestors who once lived in healthy nations where everybody had dignity and stood for what's right as a normal way of life. This was the only way humans lived for millions of years. So what happened to cause so many people to tolerate abusive behavior? Why do so many people pretend things are fine when they're not, or blame poor people for problems caused by the rich, or accept living a meaningless life?

Imagine, again, if you were a king and wanted to conquer free people and train them for submissive obedience. You could torture and kill disobedient adults to scare the rest into submission, but the adults all grew up with a basically respectful childhood so they have dignity and high self-worth. The adults know what it's like to have deep integrity and trust and to stand for a culture of mutual respect, even if it's not allowed. Even if you imposed a shaming, disconnecting, pro-obedience religion, few would accept it.

But what if you could instill deep shame, low self-worth, and all manner of emotional dysfunction on people from a very young age so that they didn't have the spiritual strength to stand for what's right in adulthood? People who have been mistreated or deprived in childhood are likely to grow up and somehow mistreat their own children, knowingly or not. An endless cycle is maintained in which each generation trains the next to have strange emotional disturbances and feel hurtful qualities like shame, selfishness, disconnection, low awareness, or low self-worth.

Unfortunately, many ruling classes have recognized this truth, and this explains why forcibly kidnapping and abusing children has often been a key element in conquering previously-free people. It also explains why ongoing, widespread child abuse and deprivation are essential to maintaining support for abusive rulers in unhealthy nations across the centuries.

The Lakota and Nootka offer tragic examples, as they were ultimately unable to prevent conquering Christians from kidnapping most of their children and sending them to abusive boarding schools.

Lakota children experienced many years of abuse at the Carlisle Indian Industrial School in the United States, where physical and sexual abuse was common. Girls and boys were shamed and humiliated and trained to hate their healthy nation. One man named White Hat said, "I was so angry that I was born an Indian that I didn't want to live."[112]

At boarding schools, children encountered many forms of child abuse. They were forced to do work they often found meaningless or boring, unlike their traditional upbringing that emphasized always walking a meaningful, enlivening path. Ohiyesa hinted at his boredom when he wrote, "I hardly think I was ever tired in my life until those first days of boarding-school." Instead of being trained to protect and provide for his people, he was now continuously given meaningless schoolwork, "until not a semblance of our native dignity and self-respect was left."[65]

At Catholic boarding schools, Nootka girls learned to feel intense shame and believe that once a month they became filthy. The boys were taught that women were dirty and sinful, had no valuable opinions, and only existed to serve men. When the children were finally allowed home, the Nootka mothers "saw the fighting and the drunkenness where once there was love and respect. They saw men beating their wives and children. They saw mothers beating their children and even abandoning them. They saw girls who should have been clan mothers become prostitutes in the cities the invaders built."[38]

The Haudenosaunee[203], Potawatomi[126] and many other healthy nations suffered this way. Endless stories of child abuse in Catholic boarding schools from around the world tell a similar tale: child abuse and deprivation trains children to tolerate and perpetuate hurtful behavior, and this serves ruling classes as emotionally troubled, shame-filled people lack the spiritual strength to stand in solidarity to stop their abuse.

Some Lakota and Nootka were thankfully able to maintain much of their ancient wisdom through the terrible boarding school period and ongoing enforced poverty, and still stand in solidarity with the Earth today. But their experiences show that it only took a single generation for terrible troubles like drunkenness, shame, and domestic violence to take hold that seem so tragically widespread in every unhealthy nation. This proves again that humans didn't "evolve" to live in unhealthy nations; we have to be trained for it, and a key aspect of this training involves difficult childhoods that result in emotional and spiritual wounds that many people struggle with their whole lives.

This shows that the transition out of "traditional times" involved being conquered. And what does "being conquered" mean? In practice, it means other people impose laws on you and choose how they're enforced, and you must obey. That fundamentally is the way of life in all unhealthy nations. People don't choose their laws, may not enforce their own laws, and must obey the laws they're given. All unhealthy nations are nations of conquered, unfree people.

While every instance of conquering is unique, they are all similarly traumatic. That means your ancestors went through something just as traumatic as the Nootka and Lakota. Your ancestors went through it decades, centuries, or maybe millennia ago, and if you don't remember those stories, it's only because those stories are no longer passed down. Thus drug and alcohol abuse, despair, depression, domestic violence, and the other widespread troubles may now seem normal or "just how life is."

But just because you are not aware of what your ancestors went through does not mean it did not happen. Those ancient traumas were never fully healed, and they still affect us today.

Child Abuse Profoundly Affects Our Politics Today

Mistreatment of children has a profound effect on our politics, because people's childhood experiences radically affect their spirituality – that is, childhood experiences dramatically affect how people relate to themselves and the world. An abused or deprived child can struggle to trust others or themselves, or cultivate deep rage, resentment, shame, sense of isolation, fear, stress, or other troubles that color the rest of their lives if they're unable to heal.

The *True Americanism* study interviewed 40 American men, 25 who volunteered to fight in the Vietnam war and 15 who took a stand to end that war, even at great personal risk. The large majority of war volunteers had grown up in traditional American families that researchers characterized as "conformistic," "emotionally isolated," and "autocratic," with adults emotionally lashing out at children while demanding respect in return, and even some physical abuse. The large majority of war-resisters grew up in households that researchers described as "warm," "gentle," and "friendly."[167,164]

The differences in adulthood were profound. The war volunteers were aware they obeyed corrupt political leaders and were just cogs in a machine, and they were ok with this, telling the researchers things like, "somebody has got to be the cog in the wheel..." and "many people have got their thumb in the pie over there..." and "it doesn't matter to me why we're fighting or where we're fighting. It's my job as a soldier..."[163]

These men clearly had learned to ignore their own dignity and sense of right and wrong. They were not offering their sacred gifts. Instead of living the most meaningful life imaginable, they were willing to be cogs in a machine they knew was corrupt.[163]

In contrast, the war-resisters had the spiritual strength to oppose an unjust war even at great personal risk, with almost all of them either having been imprisoned, awaiting sentencing or facing trial at the time of their interviews. Growing up in respectful settings, they cultivated the self-respect to stand for what's right in adulthood. But the differences in these two groups of men go deeper still.[166]

When children are repeatedly mistreated or deprived, they can learn to "hold back" or "shut down" parts of themselves, ignoring certain feelings, urges, and observations and developing hurtful attitudes in order to numb the pain of continual dissatisfaction. People can then learn to ignore that they're doing these things, making the protective behaviors and attitudes subconscious. When this is severe enough, it can lead to adults with very disturbing attitudes and behavior. Many adults struggle to feel any pleasure or connection at all, or even reject many kinds of affectionate physical pleasure.[224,223]

Interviewers found that most war-volunteers were unable to feel deeply, describing relationships as a "burden." Investigating the war-volunteers' youth, researchers found that "the first act of sexual intercourse was emotionally and interpersonally insignificant to nearly all the boys." Only 5 out of 25 had any kind of emotional response. Of these five, two felt satisfied, one felt disappointed, and two of these five men felt disgust at their first sex. In adulthood, many war-volunteers sought sexual partners whom they described as "sluts, whores, easy lay," and researchers said, "superficiality and insincerity were the only stable emotional features of their response to women. There were almost no signs of guilt, embarrassment, reflection or self-criticism in their accounts of their activities."[160]

In contrast, the war-resisters valued sexual relationships based on good communication and emotional openness. Most men had not exhibited these qualities in early sexual encounters and felt regret, saying they had lost out on chances for personal growth. Many described having learned lessons from women sexual partners, including how to relate to people, share, and enjoy life.[161,162]

Abusive or deprived childhoods profoundly affect people's capacity for pleasure and connection, with some people unable to feel deeply in adulthood and even rejecting deep pleasure and connection as a "burden." In other words, these war-volunteers were *not able* to feel certain feelings. They lacked a capacity that seems inherent or normal to people raised in a respectful way. They weren't necessarily taught to objectify women and embrace double standards. Child abuse can train children to have insecurity and little or no empathy. Of course someone who doesn't feel deeply is more likely to treat others like objects, i.e. objectifying them. And insecure people tend to put others down.

Even if ruling classes didn't manipulate elections, how are people supposed to agree on any political issues when some people value pleasure, connection and having a meaningful life, and others embrace superficiality and allow themselves to be cogs in a machine?

When children are trained for obedience, and child abuse and deprivation can cause strong insecurities, is it any wonder that cowardice is common in adulthood, and people have low trust in each other?

Child abuse or deprivation aren't all-or-nothing. Some people grow up with far more than others, and nearly all of us raised in unhealthy nations carry at least some negative impacts from our childhood. Some kinds of child abuse become normalized, encouraged, and even legally required, such as forcing children to obey unaccountable authorities and tolerate meaningless or boring work in school so that they will obediently tolerate meaningless jobs in adulthood.

These emotional troubles can also make it difficult to have satisfying romantic and spousal relationships, limiting the connection and trust many people experience even in their families.

The war-resisters had grown up with a respectful childhood, so respect was the norm for them. They grew up with the spiritual strength needed to oppose an unjust war. The war-volunteers grew up in disrespectful homes with troubles such as double standards, little loving touch, and emotional and physical abuse. In adulthood, they tolerated being cogs in a machine.

This is *not* to say that "warriors are bad" or "war resistance is good." A nation must always be ready to defend itself. The question is whether or not people are emotionally capable of having integrity and deep relationships. Clearly when children are unable to heal from their abuse or deprivation, they can become adults willing to support disrespectful authorities.

Of course, not everyone trained for obedience becomes obedient. Some become people-pleasers, and others become self-centered. Every childhood is unique, and each child responds to their challenges in their own way. People can develop many hurtful attitudes from disrespectful childhoods when they're unable to heal.

Abused people commonly abuse their children, and even many parents who mean well still act disrespectfully in ways they do not see due to their own emotional troubles. When adults are not allowed to set good boundaries by standing for what's right, many people never learn to set healthy boundaries even in their personal lives, and thus struggle to set kind and firm boundaries with their children, which causes them to struggle. This is only compounded by the stresses many parents feel due to financial insecurity, relationship troubles, and other challenges. In this way, each generation trains the next to have emotional troubles that, over time, effectively train people to tolerate a disrespectful nation.

This shows how conquering is not a single event, but a continual process involving rampant child abuse. Child abuse is a core characteristic of every unhealthy nation that allows it to persist, generation after generation. That means *treating children respectfully is essential to creating healthy nations*.

Unfortunately, deep training for submissive obedience does not end in childhood, but continues throughout adulthood. How are adults trained to tolerate abusive behavior all around them?

When Adults Learn to "Hold Back" or "Shut Down" Parts of Themselves

Julian Assange said how people learn to tolerate abuse: "Every time we witness an injustice and do not act, we train our character to be passive in its presence and thereby eventually lose all ability to defend ourselves and those we love."[14]

What qualities would people need to cultivate to have the strength to live in a healthy nation? And how are adults trained to tolerate living in an unhealthy nation with widespread exploitation?

- *Low-integrity instead of high integrity:* Every human has an urge to stand for what's right in solidarity with others, but this isn't allowed in unhealthy nations where people are expected to obey the law but not uphold it. When people learn to ignore injustice or feel helpless to stop it, life can seem meaningless, and low integrity becomes common.

- *Cowardice instead of bravery:* When the police punish anyone who takes a stand against abusive authorities, they arrest the bravest people and scare the rest into holding back, tolerating abuse, and focusing on their own comfort and safety. When bravery is punished, cowardice becomes common.

- *Selfishness instead of generosity:* Profit economies reward selfish, profit-seeking behavior rather than generosity.

- *Resentment instead of gratitude:* When people live in financial desperation, learn to fear or resent their neighbors, learn to tolerate injustice, struggle with childhood emotional wounds, and do not know how to receive the gifts of the Earth, it is easy to feel resentment instead of gratitude for the gifts of life.

- *Disconnection instead of connection with people:* When authorities propagate racist, sexist, or hateful attitudes, punish people for upholding their own law, and sabotage solidarity movements, it becomes difficult to have trusting and meaningful connections with many other people.

- *Disconnection instead of connection with nature:* Profit economies force people to seek money to survive, rather than build a mutually enriching relationship with the Earth.

- *Displeasure instead of pleasure:* Many people who are deprived of abundant loving touch in childhood may feel displeasure, dissatisfaction or disconnection as a normal, baseline experience of life and struggle to feel deep pleasure. And many religions discourage pleasure.

- *Forgetting instead of remembering:* Everybody has ancestors who lived in healthy nations in the past, but most have forgotten and think their unhealthy nation is "just how life is."

- *Shame instead of dignity:* Authoritarian religions train people to feel shame, disconnection from the divinity of life around and within us, belief in inherent badness or selfishness, displeasure, low self-worth, and other negative qualities.

- *Ignorance instead of awareness:* Unhealthy nations often propagate hurtful racist or sexist assumptions, or rigid ideologies and dogmas about how life "should be," whether in economics, religion, or politics. Lazy or rigid thinking makes people easy to manipulate, so deep awareness is rare.

Many Christians are willing to believe that people are sinful and the world is sinful because qualities like dishonesty, selfishness, and cowardice are so widespread. The truth is that these hurtful qualities are only widespread in unhealthy nations because authorities create conditions that reward selfishness, discourage deep integrity and bravery, and punish those who stand for justice no matter what.

Childhood emotional wounds can cause a lifetime of significant unease, insecurity, or feeling of inherent badness which colors the way many people see the world. When such wounded children grow up around widespread selfishness, dishonesty, and cowardice, is it any wonder humans may seem inherently sinful?

However, no one is inherently bad, selfish or hateful. Hurtful qualities like selfishness or cowardice are not our nature as humans. They have to be trained.

We Are Continually Reconquered

For millions of years, every child was trained for beautiful qualities, in part so they would have the strength to stand for a culture of mutual respect in solidarity with others. Only in recent times have people been trained otherwise.

And what is the result? *Abusive behavior is pervasive.*

To maintain this way of life, we are continually reconquered: our bravest, wisest, and most generous spiritual leaders are attacked or killed. We are trapped in financial desperation and surrounded by deceit in the news media. Authoritarian religions train people to obey corrupt leaders. Leaders propagate racist, sexist, and hateful attitudes, and force poor people to fight their wars so the rich get even richer. Solidarity movements are continually sabotaged. Pollution and economic "development" poison and scar the living world that we're all part of. Selfishness is rewarded throughout the economy. And ongoing widespread childhood deprivation and abuse trains many people to support all this or resist ineffectively in countless different ways.

It is Time to End this Pervasive Abuse

Ending this abuse will require creating new healthy nations, one community at a time, where *everyone agrees on the laws and everyone bravely upholds them, taking humans' and nonhumans' needs into account.*

After a shallow revolution, one ruling class takes over from another and for most people, nothing much changes. After the Deepest Revolution there will be no ruling class, as each person stands in solidarity with everyone else, fully embracing the golden rule.

You and the people around you can do this. Explore paths to creating a new healthy nation in *Part 3 - The Deepest Revolution*.

Part 3

The Deepest Revolution

Chapter 15: The Biggest Secret in Human History

What do you think is the biggest secret in human history?

What secret has been kept from billions of people across every continent going back centuries or even millennia?

The most widespread and ancient secret is this: you could potentially live in a nation that maintains a respectful way of life among the people, and between the people and the Earth. That means we don't need unaccountable politicians to be tough on crime – we could live without crime. We don't need to vote for the lesser evil – we could have leaders that the whole nation trusts. We don't need to work unsatisfying jobs, be distrustful of our neighbors, and suffer all kinds of discrimination and financial stress while the rich keep getting richer.

We could have a way of life where trust is normal because integrity and generosity are normal too. Many nations around the world, now and in the recent past, show that this is not just possible, but the normal and healthy way for humans to live.

Why has this been such an epic, widely-kept secret? Of course: *this is what it's like to live in freedom*. However, ruling classes consistently train their conquered subjects to think they're already free so they won't see how much better life could be. For centuries, conquered people have been kept ignorant of the existence of healthy nations that show what freedom is like, or they've been trained to misunderstand them.

When you know what to look for, the history books show this vividly.

Just as the American, German, and other authorities are falsely calling anti-genocide protesters "antisemitic" today and using that as an excuse to punish them, for centuries European colonial authorities likewise have falsely called people of healthy nations "ignorant", "savages," "uneducated," and "the antichrist." Centuries of lies and manipulation in North and South America, Africa, Australia, and around the world trained conquered people to fear and hate free people of healthy nations instead of seeing them as potential mentors, allies, and friends.[228] Chapter 2 showed that sometimes the secret got out, and some colonists did indeed run away to live in freedom.

Why would ruling classes work so hard to spread propaganda against healthy nations? David Mantell, author of the *True Americanism* study, said it clearly: "It is difficult to live in a permanent state of rebellion, and rebellions rarely occur when people do not have standards of comparison or do not see the chance of changing their circumstances."[165]

Ruling classes try to keep people in despair, not knowing that another way of life is possible without corruption, discrimination, and greed.

But now you know the secret. You know that we're not free now, and you know what freedom is like. You know that it's possible to live in a beautiful way, without all the cultural and political problems that can seem "just the way life is."

Most people either haven't heard of healthy nations or they misunderstand them, so they have no standard of comparison, and they're likely to accept their unhealthy nation as "good enough." British prime minister Winston Churchill even said, "democracy is the worst form of government except for all those other forms that have been tried..."[46]

Of course, if you believe the only alternative to authoritarian democracy is being ruled by a king, priest or imam, then you'll do your best to make democracy "work."

But what if you learned what freedom is like by studying people who are truly free? And what if you found examples from today or recent times, including case studies of successful revolutionary movements?

What if you realized how much your unhealthy nation had trained you and your ancestors to hold back your deepest love and tolerate predatory behavior all around you?

And what if you could see that it doesn't need to be this way, that you and other strong and caring people could unite to create a new nation where respect is the norm?

At that moment, everything changes. *The secret is out!*

Once you know what healthy nations are like, you have that standard of comparison. You can see that *voting will never lead to deep change because slaves have never voted their way to freedom.* You can see that endless debates between left and right, liberals and conservatives, and capitalists and socialists are distractions from the conversations and actions that might lead to the Deepest Revolution.

Instead of engaging in unproductive political debates, what if you imagined the kind of world you wanted to live in? And what if you worked with others to bring your vision to life?

Imagine...

Imagine having amazing friends who tell the truth, share, keep their promises, and support you in difficult times, and who expect the same from you.

Imagine choosing to live with those friends so you're surrounded by neighbors you deeply trust, and who trust you.

Imagine a life where every moment feels alive, and you are free to contribute to your community in the most meaningful ways without worrying if it pays well or at all.

Imagine a world with no police or prisons, where no one worries about crime because you know that if anyone misbehaves or threatens you, your friends and neighbors will come to your aid. Just like you would for them.

Imagine having enough time with your kids and having enough time to make their education really excellent, so that every day is meaningful and engaging for them. Imagine training children for qualities like integrity, generosity, awareness, bravery, and joy so that these become normal parts of their lives and pervasive in your nation.

Imagine no boring classes, no unaccountable school authorities, and no meaningless work and tests that train children for meaningless work in adulthood. Instead, imagine being a teenager and being treated so respectfully that there is nothing to rebel against.

Imagine going through a process where your nation chooses a leader, and people like Jesus Christ or Martin Luther King Jr are selected.

Imagine finding your childhood innocence again, joyfully offering your deepest love in each moment surrounded by other people giving theirs. Because of course no one loses their innocence. When people embrace hurtful qualities like shame, low self-worth, or selfishness, and learn to hold back their deepest love, *people forget their innocence.*

And anything that's been forgotten can be remembered again.

Can you imagine if people took care of their neighborhoods instead of tolerating trash and pollution, as people with dignity and self-respect likewise respect the space where they live?

Imagine working with your neighbors to take care of everyone's needs together, with no need to worry about health care, retirement, having shelter or enough to eat – and you don't need to work an unsatisfying job to maybe have enough money to pay for it all!

Imagine seeing gifts everywhere you look, and feeling a continuous state of joyful gratitude for all of life's blessings.

Imagine feeling indebted because your neighbors give you so much that you constantly feel the urge to give back, with the endless sharing just adding to the joyful feeling of indebtedness. Who would want to wipe clean such happy debts?

Imagine befriending animals like the deer and bear, trees like the chestnuts and hickories, and herbs like nettle and chickweed, and learning how to feed their communities just as they feed yours. Imagine knowing the plants and animals so intimately that you increase their populations even as you respectfully harvest them.

No one can predict or control the future. Times of sickness or hunger might come, or war and migration. Imagine trusting that the people around you will take care of you, just like you'll take care of them. Imagine relaxing into that "realization that people and community are there to sustain you [which] creates the most secure feeling in the world..."[183]

None of this is theoretical or idealistic. Every scene you just imagined came from a story or observation from real people like you and me in an actual healthy nation.

This incredible vision is not a fantasy. You and other people can bring this vision to life.

Will You Bring Your Vision to Life or Let it Die?

All these things you just imagined created a beautiful vision. You could work with other people to bring your vision to life, or you could forget it.

I want to tell you the story of someone who chose to forget. Their story showed me how easy it is to forget, and it taught me how to keep a beautiful vision alive.

I know someone who, in the early 1990s, thought about whether it was ok for the US to invade Iraq. She had never engaged in politics much, but as the United States invaded, she wondered, is the US really invading to bring democracy like the politicians say? Or is the real purpose to take Iraq's oil? Is it ok to kill people to take oil?

These were very deep questions.

Unfortunately, she was unable to find people to share her concerns with and speak her heart. Her husband and friends were involved with the war and seemed unwilling to question it. She was surrounded by people but felt alone, unable to discuss her thoughts and fears, and unable to consider how to respond with others.

Over time, she became more stressed, and she and her husband began speaking of divorce. She had the career and family of her dreams but was unhappy and felt stuck and alone. Finally, she decided to take antidepressants, which allowed her to numb the feeling of dissatisfaction without bravely responding to it. And she stopped asking such deep questions about her unhealthy nation.

A person who doesn't have anyone to share their thoughts and feelings with can easily feel trapped, unable to respond to their frustrations and fears. Many people cope by numbing their feelings with endless distractions, such as staring at their phone, focusing on superficial hobbies, taking antidepressants, drug and alcohol abuse, or overworking. These are simply ways people learn to "hold back" or "shut down" parts of themselves to avoid feeling their own dissatisfaction when they don't see a way to meaningfully respond.

This story shows how easy it can be to ignore legitimate frustrations and fears, to numb the feelings and tolerate the numbness. It also shows how important it is to *share your thoughts and feelings with trusted friends, hear theirs, and consider how to respond together.*

So find trustworthy people and tell them your thoughts and feelings, and listen to them too. When you can speak clearly with thoughtful, caring people in private, they will help you remember that you are sane, and it's your unhealthy nation that is crazy.

Revolutionary Activity #26
Find people with whom you can speak your heart

It can be extremely helpful to have thoughtful, trustworthy people to speak your heart to. If you don't know anybody you trust this much, find new friends. Your future friends are out there, and they'll be glad to meet you. If you have friends you trust, come together so you can share what is in your heart, listen to them, and respond to any concerns together.

Revolutionary Activity #27
Create private spaces

To really speak your heart with trusted friends, you need privacy. Learn how to create surveillance-free spaces so you can speak with trusted friends with no recording devices present. For example, do experiments with your phone to discover how sensitive the microphone is, and how and where it can be safely stored so you can speak freely.

Chapter 16: Build Your Spiritual Strength

So many aspects of our way of life in unhealthy nations keep us stuck. The profit economy encourages us to focus on our own needs and make money just to survive. We are trained to care about certain things and ignore others, and where to put our attention, time, and money. Many "conventional" or "mainstream" values are somehow superficial or misguided.

Growing up, I learned that the United States was the best country in the world, and I felt proud to live in a capitalist democracy. I looked forward to contributing to the United States' progress and growth throughout my life. As a church-going Christian, I bowed my head every night before dinner and prayed.

Over time, as I learned all the things that I share in this book, I had to give up a lot of beliefs – beliefs about the society I live in, beliefs about history, beliefs about myself and the future, beliefs about what matters and what doesn't matter.

Giving up old beliefs and perspectives can be hard, even when it's obvious that they don't work. Don Cox described his own transformation. He had engaged in various kinds of activism to fight racial oppression in the US, but finally in 1967 he went to a conference where black people openly discussed revolution. Cox heard Black Panthers speak for the first time. He said, "I was drunk with this new world I had not even known existed. Pieces started falling into place. It was a cascade, a snowball rolling down the mountainside."[50]

Then he described how hard this was: "Everything I had heard during the weekend helped me understand that all the efforts I had made up until then to be acceptable to mainstream society had just made me a 'good nigger.' I was simultaneously ashamed and furious. All I could do was cry." Cox eventually dedicated himself to freeing black Americans from oppression, becoming a senior leader in the Black Panthers.[50]

Bogaletch Gebre described her own powerful transformation. As a young adult, she underwent female genital mutilation in Ethiopia, being taught that it made her a "whole woman." Later in life, a friend learned of this and felt horrified, and at first Gebre defended the practice as she had for years. Then she "experienced an incredible awakening, then a tidal wave of anger, as I began to comprehend all that had been taken from me in ignorance... Tears of understanding flooded from me as I allowed the scientist in me to see, to examine in a new light, all that I remembered..." Gebre went on to lead a movement to abolish female genital mutilation.[185]

Find the Courage to Release What Doesn't Work

Giving up old beliefs is hard. Even Jesus Christ needed 40 days alone in the desert before he could fully confront the urge to seek wealth and power that his unhealthy nation instilled in him, and instead choose a path of service. After his transformation, he began a ministry that went on to inspire others for 2,000 years.

This kind of transformation seems common among activists and spiritual leaders. When you grow up in an unhealthy nation, you may be taught all kinds of hurtful or wrong things – perhaps you learned that obedience is good and people are basically bad or naturally selfish (addressed in Chapters 7 and 9), that some people are worse than others or deserve to suffer (Chapter 10), that political and religious authorities serve the people (Chapters 8, 12 and 14), or that you live in a free society (Chapter 6).

But in order for spiritual leaders like Don Cox, Jesus Christ, and Bogaletch Gebre to truly serve their people, they had to go through transformations that helped them accept the truth and release the beliefs and attitudes that they knew were not working.

Giving up old beliefs is hard, but it becomes so much easier when you begin to see a better way. It's easier to give up on "divinely-ordained" monarchy or authoritarian "democracy" when you see how free people choose their leaders. It's easier to give up submissive obedience when you see how people live freely, without fear of punishment. It's easier to trust yourself and trust others when you know how trustworthy people can be.

Embrace your curiosity, and open your mind to possibilities that may have seemed impossible before. As you free your mind from beliefs that don't work, and make space for perspectives that do, you will feel more empowered to make a difference for the people and nonhumans around you.

To live in a healthy nation, you will need to embrace a very different way of life than your unhealthy nation trained you for. A way of life without submissive obedience, with dignity instead of unacknowledged humiliation, with bravery instead of cowardice, where justice and trust are normal because integrity is normal too, where neighbors share generously and the community takes the Earth's needs into account. For a group to make this way of life real, each person will need 1) deep spiritual strength, 2) deep connections with other like-minded people, and 3) a deep connection with the Earth. *Part 3* addresses these three themes.

Revolutionary Activity #28
Release what isn't working

Reflect on your life, and think of one belief you have that isn't working. Do you keep voting, hoping someday the government won't be corrupt? Do you believe people are inclined to sin or that obedience is good? Do you have shame about your body, and so you have self-doubt or low self-worth? Do you think rich people are better than poor, and you judge people by how much money they have instead of how much they serve the people around them? Do you believe other people are basically untrustworthy, and so you struggle to form deeply trusting relationships?

Take some time and think of a belief or attitude that hasn't served you, and embrace one that might serve you better.

Cultivate Spiritual Strength, Part 1: Practice Noticing the Gifts You Receive and Feeling Grateful

Cultivating a practical, aware gratitude is the first step to build spiritual strength.

To me, a person has *spiritual strength* if they give their love fully without holding back, and if they stand for what's right for themselves and others. So what does that have to do with gratitude?

When I notice and feel gratitude for others' gifts, it makes it hard for me not to give my own gifts in turn. I didn't understand this till I began nature connection practices and feeling grateful for all the gifts I received.

I started out seeing the forest as a "green wall." I liked walking through trees, but I hardly knew anything about them or the other creatures that lived there. I would have missed the forest if it was gone, but I mostly lived inside and focused on human affairs.

But I kept going to my sit spot to observe the nonhumans, and I kept studying my field guides and reference books, and listening to my mentors' stories and suggestions. When I traveled or lived in cities, I found parks or even a back porch to practice observing every day. And I learned how to notice and receive the gifts of the Earth, so that as I walk around I see gifts everywhere I look.

The cedar and basswood trees offer me the tools to make fire, and now whenever I see these trees, I see the gift of fire, and all the fire's gifts such as warmth, cooking and camaraderie with friends.

Chestnut trees and oaks give the gifts of food, the same as herbs like chickweed or animals like deer and bear. All these give the gift of nutritious food and joyful time with friends as we respectfully harvest, process, and eat the food together.

Stinging nettle has helped me relieve joint pain, and I've witnessed lobelia used in first aid to open a person's airways when they suffered a strong allergic response and struggled to breathe.

Yucca has offered me its leaves to make rope, and miscanthus grass has helped me make a watertight roof to keep me dry.

I learned to receive intangible gifts too – the delight at seeing the sun reflect off the dew in the morning, or cooling off in a stream on a hot summer day. I was grateful to the plants I couldn't use directly, because they offered food and homes to birds and other animals that I was happy to have as company.

The more I learned to receive the Earth's gifts, and the more I practiced feeling grateful, the more I saw gifts everywhere I looked. I felt surrounded by abundance, and grateful for life.

The more I felt grateful for the living world, the harder it became to see how most humans treat it.

I kept driving past clear-cut forests, huge fields of empty clay destined to be cheap strip malls, dirty factories, and overpriced housing developments full of toxic building materials.

The more I felt the Earth's gifts in my bones, the deeper I felt the loss every time a river is polluted, or a forest is cut down.

Eventually, I just had to find ways to protect the forest. I couldn't bear to see the nonhumans I loved being killed in senseless ways.

I had an urge to protect the forest, an urge I couldn't ignore even if I wanted. I was too full of gratitude, too aware of the nonhumans' gifts to me and to each other, too aware of the divinity that lives in them just as it lives in me and all people. I couldn't ignore that desire to protect the rivers and forests I loved.

There may be many ways to cultivate passion and deep connection with others. But this deep gratitude helped me feel a love in my heart and desire to serve nonhumans I'd never experienced before. Earlier in life, I didn't give my sacred gifts to the nonhumans, and I didn't stand for what's right and protect them. Cultivating this practical, aware gratitude helped me get on a good path.

Deep gratitude can help you too. Practice noticing the gifts you receive, and practice feeling grateful. Keep practicing gratitude until it becomes your baseline approach to life, looking for beauty even in difficult moments. When you feel that urge to give back, grateful for the gifts you receive, you'll be on a good path too.

Revolutionary Activity #29
Learn to receive the tangible gifts of the Earth

Have you ever felt curious to learn how to navigate by starlight, eat wild foods, build a house of natural materials, or make fire by rubbing sticks together? Situational awareness, nutrition, housing, and fire are all examples of the endless gifts that the

Earth can provide if you learn how to gratefully receive them.

Notice any curiosity you've felt about some aspect of the nonhuman world, even going back to your childhood. Whatever it is, follow that curiosity. Learn how to make fire, forage wild foods, or wherever your curiosity guides you so that you begin to receive the gifts of the Earth.

Revolutionary Activity #30
Give thanks for the Earth's intangible gifts

Have you ever gone on a walk to get fresh air and clear your head, or gone to the woods for private time away from people? Have you ever admired the enchanting silver light of the moon at night? Imagine life without any trees or fresh air or the moon, and see how poorer that life would be.

Think of an intangible gift you receive from the Earth, whether from plants or animals or streams or anything else, and practice noticing and feeling grateful for it.

Revolutionary Activity #31
Practice the same gratitude with people

What tangible and intangible gifts do you receive from people around you? Is there a child whose smile lifts your spirits, or an older friend who has mentored you? Have family members helped you pay for school, or friends supported you during a difficult time in a relationship? Notice the gifts you receive and feel grateful for them. Express your gratitude to the people directly so they know the impact they had on you.

Cultivate Spiritual Strength, Part 2: Nurture Your Sacred Gifts and Give Them in Service of the People and Nonhumans you Love

When I study the great spiritual leaders I've found, something really stands out: it's like they are compelled to serve their people, and it would be unthinkable not to. It's as if they didn't have any choice in the matter.

Harriet Tubman was a black runaway slave during the times of US chattel slavery. When she finally reached the North, where chattel slavery was outlawed, her first thought was to return to her people and help them escape too.[31]

In the coming years, she kept going back to help others escape, over and over. She was never caught, but if she had been, she'd have been tortured with unthinkable cruelty. But she loved her people so much, she was willing to accept the risk.[31]

Tubman described the sense of being moved by a greater power very vividly. Whenever someone remarked on her courage or good fortune, she would say, "'Twan't me, 'twas de Lord! Jes' so long as he wanted to use me, he would take keer of me, an' when he didn't want me no longer, I was ready to go."[31]

Jesus Christ and Martin Luther King Jr were the same – both of them repeatedly acknowledged that they were going to die because of the ways they served their people, and yet they kept on serving in the most meaningful ways they knew how.

Like Tubman, both Martin Luther King Jr and Jesus Christ described a sense of being compelled by a higher power. Christ said he came "not to do my own will but the will of him who sent me."[73] The night before he was killed, King said, "Longevity has its place. But I'm not concerned about that now. I just want to do God's will."[138]

What is this greater power, or divine voice, that moves some people to act so selflessly even at great personal risk? And how come so few people seem to listen to it?

The truth is very simple: everyone has a divine voice in their heart that, from birth on, guides them to walk a meaningful, dignified path in service of the people and nonhumans they love. The divine voice isn't the endless mental chatter so many people experience; it feels more like a deep knowing, or even an irresistible force that guides you on your own sacred path. However, in unhealthy nations, people are subject to so much hurtful training that many learn to "hold back" or "shut down" parts of themselves, and ultimately they can learn to ignore that voice in their heart. People can learn to obediently follow others' direction instead of following their divine path. They can learn to embrace self-centeredness, low self-worth, or distrust. People can learn to tolerate meaningless work and find ways to distract themselves from the dissatisfaction of not giving their deepest love in service of others.

Tubman, King, and Christ only seem unusual because they gave their love fully in unhealthy nations that train people to hold back their love. They could feel that inner divine voice, whereas many people learn to ignore it, starting with early childhood deprivation or abuse and continuing with endless training for obedience throughout school, church and adulthood.

This is one universal spiritual truth behind the teachings of religions like Christianity, Islam, and Buddhism: everyone has sacred gifts to give, a divine purpose that only they can fulfill. And the divine voice inside you already knows that purpose, whether you consciously know it or not.

There is good news: if you are like me, and you learned to hold back your love or not discover your own sacred gifts or deep purpose, there are ways to access that part of yourself so that you can give yourself fully, as did Tubman, King, and Christ. It's not complicated; it is a matter of releasing all distractions and temptations, and instead really listening to that divine voice inside you.

Some years ago, I felt stuck in life, so I decided to do a special fast alone in the woods. I had no water, no food, and no distractions – no digital devices, no reading, nothing for 92 hours.

I spent most of the time feeling stressed, because I was so used to having distractions like my job, reading the news, even nervous eating. In other words, it took awhile to calm down and just be with that inner voice that I'd learned to ignore.

Before the fast, I often felt stressed, and it was difficult for me to savor sensual pleasures. I rarely even tasted my food, as I commonly read news articles or watched videos while I ate. I'd learned to distract myself from the deep dissatisfaction I was feeling.

I had no great insight during this fast. I just slowly calmed down. I never felt hungry, and only occasionally felt thirsty. I knew from previous fasting what it's like to eat or drink out of nervousness, so I knew not to worry, and my thirst quickly went away.

Finally I ended the fast with some herbal tea. As I savored the tea, I thought about how I would normally read or watch a video while drinking, and I was filled with revulsion. The thought of distracting myself from my own meaningful experience was terrible, even though just four days earlier it had seemed entirely normal.

This fast showed me how much I distracted myself from my own feelings, and how disconnected I was from that inner voice. Instead of walking a meaningful path, I was walking a comfortable path that didn't feel very meaningful, and I had learned to distract myself from my resulting dissatisfaction. The fast showed me how transformative it could be to simply release all distractions and connect with that inner divine voice.

In a sense, it felt like I was just "being myself," but I wasn't doing whatever I was used to doing, or doing whatever I felt like. I was being my deepest self, connected with that inner voice that would never tolerate meaningless distractions.

It is essential to get rid of all distractions so that you can hear that divine voice, as many spiritual leaders have shown. Jesus Christ famously began his ministry immediately after fasting for 40 days alone in the desert, where he confronted temptations to become wealthy and powerful, and instead chose a path of service.[198]

Ohiyesa described how, among the traditional Sioux, praying alone in the wilderness "was customary with the best young men."[70]

Apache man Stalking Wolf described how the vision quest "provides all the answers to life, to spirit," and it "brings forth the pure self untainted by any and all outside distractions," and ultimately "gives us a Vision, a command from the Creator, and a grand purpose to life."[32]

"Command from Creator," "divine voice," "sacred gifts," and "deepest love" are all ways of saying the same thing. That divine voice is inside you right now, and it's waiting for you to listen so you can walk your divine path and offer your own sacred gifts, or your deepest love. All it takes is the courage to release distractions and feel that deepest part of you that others in your unhealthy nation haven't always welcomed.

You matter, and there's a reason you're alive. You have sacred gifts, special ways of making the world a better place that only you can give. Any time you don't give your gifts, the world becomes poorer.

Commit to discovering and giving your own sacred gifts, and living the most meaningful life imaginable in service of the people and nonhumans you love.

There are many ways to discover and give your gifts, as Chapter 3 described: you could learn how to fast safely in nature and spend time away from people without distraction, including without news and digital entertainments. Notice what sparks special joy or curiosity in your life. Ask friends to tell you when they've seen you be the most joyful and engaged. Notice your anger, and let that anger show you what you care about, and how you might act in service. If you choose to fast, I recommend the book *Fasting Can Save Your Life* by Herbert Shelton.

In unhealthy nations that train people for a life of distraction, any practice that helps you avoid distraction can help reconnect you with that divine voice within you so that you can give your sacred gifts in life. These are life-long practices too, which will serve you well anytime you feel lost or stuck.

Revolutionary Activity #32
Discover your sacred gifts or your most meaningful path
Choose a time in the near future when you can avoid all distractions and feel into your heart to sense what most matters to you, or how you could give your deepest love. Practice listening with curiosity, as you don't choose your sacred gifts – they choose you.

If you do not get a clear answer quickly, have patience.

Cultivate Spiritual Strength, Part 3: Live in Reciprocity

Cultivating a practical aware gratitude and giving your sacred gifts are the first and second core spiritual practices. They're the first two steps of cultivating a deep spiritual strength.

The third core spiritual practice, living in reciprocity, completes the puzzle.

Many people practice gratitude. But if you don't give your sacred gifts from that place of gratitude, then it's not fully satisfying.

And some people cultivate passion, but if it's not offered in gratitude to the humans and nonhumans you love, what good is it?

Some people find passion for abstract things like scientific research, engineering, and writing. But when people merely enjoy their work and do not pay attention to the consequences of the work their bosses order them to do, terrible things happen. Physicists may love physics and help create weapons their rulers use in ways they later regret. Civil engineers may obsess about building codes and construct well-built prisons that corrupt legal systems use to unjustly persecute activists and the poor.

Gratitude without service can feel empty, and passion without that clear gratitude can easily become comfortable and ultimately meaningless. Ruling classes are only too happy for wage slaves to feel passionate about their jobs.

It's the 3rd core spiritual practice that ultimately ties them all together, yielding a deep spiritual strength: living in reciprocity.

When you're grateful to other people and nonhumans, and you feel an unstoppable urge to act in service, everything changes. And when those other people and nonhumans need and expect your sacred gifts, or your deepest love, magic happens.

Everything matters.

Harriet Tubman faced extreme risk as she worked to free enslaved people. This meant that every aspect of preparation and execution was extremely important. She was fully aware of the risks, and she conveyed this importance to the people she rescued.[31]

For example, Tubman brought a gun, not only to protect herself from slavecatchers and their dogs, but also to keep the group together. The way was so difficult that men would sometimes give up, their feet sore and bleeding, claiming they could not take another step. They would say they were ready to die, or if their strength returned, go back to their old home. In order to protect the whole group from the torture and endless oppression they would face if they were caught, Tubman would point her revolver at the head of the exhausted man and say, "Dead niggers tell no tales; you go on or die!" Thus she ensured nobody betrayed the group, even accidentally, and made it possible for everyone to escape safely.[31]

As they escaped together, everyone needed to fully meet their potential and do their very best. Everything mattered, and Tubman held them to the highest standards as an act of love. By setting firm boundaries, she helped the men find their strength.

A story from the Zapatistas shows how every moment matters, even in moments of joyful calm. Your energy ripples out into the world. Just as your presence can lift others' spirits, any emotional disconnection, carelessness, or unawareness can likewise affect other people's energy around you. Okhi Forest and her young daughter visited the Zapatistas, and her daughter once dropped a broom on the ground without thinking about it. A Zapatista woman gently encouraged her daughter, "Don't drop the broom carelessly like that, you can really affect a lot of people!"[188]

It's not that every moment becomes "serious" or stressful; it's simply an attitude that the world is alive, and every moment is a gift not to be missed or taken for granted. When you give your deepest love you inspire others to give theirs, and when you hold back, this affects other people too.

Your love could light up the world, but it's hard to keep giving alone. And it's hard to give if you don't feel very grateful.

When you cultivate deep relationships, where each person is grateful for the other's gifts, something magical happens. It becomes unthinkable to give less than your fullest love, as that's simply what people expect of each other in deep relationships. And of course, it's satisfying to give your love to people who are grateful for it.

But how to form such deeply trusting, reciprocal relationships, where people share their gifts generously, and feel grateful for the gifts they receive?

All the revolutionary activities in this book are meant to help you generate exactly these kinds of relationships. When you practice keen awareness and question your assumptions, you will begin to really see other people for who they are, and who doesn't like being deeply seen by a caring person?

When you practice standing for what's right and supporting others who take a stand, you'll show courage that inspires trust in others – and who doesn't want to trust their friends?

When you practice giving first without expecting anything in return, your innocent generosity will inspire the same in others, who will know they can give to you and trust that over time you'll share too.

When you practice noticing the gifts of the nonhumans and develop mutual relationships with them, you'll make more nonhuman friends than you ever imagined.

When you cultivate deep relationships, they will give life a meaning all on their own. Your sacred gifts always matter, but you'll feel more energy to give them when there are grateful people and nonhumans to receive them.

A person has spiritual strength if they give their love fully in each moment without holding back, and if they stand for what's right for themselves and others. If you really commit to cultivating a practical aware gratitude, walking the most meaningful path, and living in reciprocity, you'll find that spiritual strength that seems so elusive in unhealthy nations.

You Are a Messiah

One of the biggest lies in history is that there is only one messiah. Christians have waited thousands of years for Jesus Christ to return and "save them," a passive attitude that only benefits oppressors.

"Messiah" just means savior or liberator, someone who helps free people from oppression.[175] Tubman, Christ, and King were all messiahs, each serving their people in their own way. In healthy nations, everyone stands for justice in one way or another, therefore *everyone* is a messiah.

And since everyone is a messiah, you are a messiah too. You may not feel ready to cultivate your spiritual power, or perhaps you feel too busy or afraid. There's a reason authoritarian religions encourage shame and low self-worth, schools train children for cowardly obedience, politicians and the media keep people divided and scared, and profit economies keep workers busy and stressed. We're trained to be slaves with a life of stress and distraction, afraid of our spiritual power. These troubles also make it hard to form reciprocal relationships with people and the Earth.

The distractions are real, but so is the divine voice speaking to you right now, as it has since your birth. This divine voice isn't separate from you; each one of us is divinity in human form, and that includes you. If you're like most people, you've only learned to hold back or shut down parts of your divine self in order to survive in your unhealthy nation.

Focusing on your survival or comfort is ultimately unsatisfying. Instead, cultivate your spiritual strength. Give your deepest love and stand for what's right as a normal way of life.

The world wants to be blessed by the light of your love.

Revolutionary Activity #33
Make spiritual growth a regular and lifelong practice

Religions like Christianity and Islam encourage people to gather at least weekly to study their religious teachings as a lifelong practice. Make your spiritual growth likewise a regular, intentional, lifelong practice. Find exercises or opportunities to practice things like bravery, gratitude, joy, integrity, humility, generosity, compassion, and awareness so they become your normal, baseline approach to life. In moments when you need to take a stand for what's right, you'll have the necessary spiritual strength because you practice that strength regularly. The activities in this book can help.

Chapter 17: Build a Healthy Nation One Community at a Time

Can you imagine your life if everyone around you could be trusted to take care of each other and to consistently stand for what's right no matter what? Where resources are freely shared and you never have to worry about affording food, shelter, or help when you need it most?

Okanagan Jeannette Armstrong called this deep trust of knowing your community is there to sustain you "the most secure feeling in the world."[183]

People in healthy nations deliberately create and maintain this secure feeling by consistently holding themselves and each other to high standards that benefit individuals because they benefit the group. They routinely expect themselves and others to behave with integrity, generosity, awareness, physical resilience, and bravery. When people make mistakes, they help each other grow without guilt or shame. When qualities like integrity and generosity become widespread, trust naturally becomes widespread too.

Healthy nations are built on healthy communities where people have deep relationships with each other and the Earth. The Zapatistas show how to build a healthy nation one community at a time.

Build a Healthy Nation One Community at a Time

Instead of instituting a new overarching government, even after their revolution, the Zapatistas said clearly that the communities are "the core of all autonomy." They formed higher levels of councils to help the communities protect each other and share resources, but no "higher ups" interfere in the communities.[199] Top-level leaders really are merely conduits for the will of the people, not dictators.

For this way of life to work, healthy communities must first exist where people hold themselves and others to high standards so they can deeply trust each other. Mexican towns existed before the revolution, but with corrupt leaders and divisive politics, they were not suitable places to discuss how to make a new healthy nation.

To help form new healthy communities, the Zapatistas traveled around to meet people face to face. Major Ana Maria described secretly hosting study sessions where people discussed how they could organize, learn and contribute.[212]

Zapatista women commanders Ramona and Susana traveled to dozens of communities where they read out the proposed Revolutionary Women's Law to women's groups. A women's group in each community gave feedback and ultimately had to approve the law to ensure that women would be fully respected in this new nation. Thousands of indigenous women were consulted.[79,170]

How could the women have offered feedback and given their consent if the women's groups didn't exist in the first place? How could the study sessions have occurred if everyone in a given town were selfishly focused on their own life, and didn't care about building a healthy nation with others?

If the communities of receptive people didn't exist, there would have been no one for the organizers to consult with or build a nation with. The respectful communities had to exist before they could be united into a respectful nation.

These healthy communities are groups of people that have their own agreements on how to live well together. They still live under ruling-class laws, but despite that, they have their own standards and choose their own way of life the best they can based on all the principles in this book, including integrity, generosity, and deep connection with the Earth.

The Zapatistas described how these healthy communities were absolutely essential for their revolution.

Commander Ramona and major Ana Maria went to live in the jungle with dedicated revolutionaries in the 1980s, where they learned key skills like hunting and fighting and gained political consciousness. They joined at the age of about 13, but accepted responsibilities as full adults and were obviously held to very high standards. At the age of 25, Ana Maria successfully led about a thousand people in a military assault to free a town from Mexican rule and Ramona directed the resulting peace negotiations.[239,170]

Many other Zapatistas didn't change their lives as much as these women and other men did; they seemed to live normal lives in Mexico but they still supported the revolution, and Ana Maria said these people played a vital role. The full-time revolutionaries had to have the support of the people to address challenges like helping them move around, get supplies, recruit, and blend in. Without the support of healthy communities of people who already had strong relationships with each other and the Earth, the revolution would have failed.[239]

What would happen if there was a revolutionary movement to create a new healthy nation, and a representative came to your region? Would there be a community of people who are already receptive to what he or she has to say because they've already been cultivating strong relationships with each other and the Earth, and they already want to live in a healthy nation? If the representative hosted a study session, would anybody come? Or would they move on, seeking more receptive people elsewhere?

It might seem hopeless to just gather a group of 5 or 10 people willing to build a different way of life together. Sure, you could be good to each other and serve the Earth locally, but maybe it seems impossible to form enough trust relationships to build a nation of many thousands or more.

But if you can help create a community of 5, 10, or 50 people, it will be part of the fertile ground from which the Deepest Revolution will sprout. When organizers come around to recruit, offer training, give and receive mutual aid, and seek input on the new nation's laws, any community you help build will play an important role. And that community must exist first.

This is what it means to *build a healthy nation one community at a time*. When you can form deep friendships with people who commit to supporting each other and the Earth, bringing out the best in each other and living a meaningful life every day, you're forming a little healthy community where trust and gratitude are the norm, because integrity and generosity are normal too.

When people feel isolated and scared, even if they don't like the corruption of their unhealthy nation, they will support and protect it because it offers them stability and some measure of safety and comfort. Their friends and family are all part of the unhealthy nation, and all their hopes and dreams are tied up in it. When a revolution occurs, people who don't have those deep relationships will easily be convinced by deceitful politicians that their way of life is under attack, and they will fight the revolutionaries.

If you can form a little community that embraces these healthy-nation practices of deep solidarity and generosity, the people in your group won't be isolated anymore. Scary things might happen, but nobody in the community will face them alone. When people can orient to this community of deep relationships, they will have less motivation to protect their unhealthy nation in order to protect themselves. Instead they will enjoy that most secure feeling in the world when they trust their community to protect them.

Over time if we can form enough healthy communities, someday they may unite to form a healthy nation, or even many nations.

Healthy communities are the building blocks of healthy nations. If you could attend one of those sessions and discuss how to form a healthy community, what do you think you might learn?

Revolutionary Activity #34
Serve the Earth Together

People can have unity when they all deeply care about the same things. This is part of the magic of the Haudenosaunee's Thanksgiving Address – among other things, it's a public statement where they remind themselves of their shared gratitude for the Earth, and how important the Earth is to them.

Build unity with others by caring for the Earth together. Whether you're protecting a forest or river from destruction or pollution, or enriching the soil or creating new bird habitat, find a practical way to work with others to give back to the nonhumans who give us humans so much.

Building a Healthy Community Starts with You

Like a healthy nation, in a healthy community people have high standards for themselves and others. Trust becomes normal because qualities like integrity, generosity, and compassion are widespread and normal too. If you've completed the revolutionary activities, you are well on your way to building a healthy community with others. Consider how the activities have helped you grow.

You've practiced standing for what's right and supporting others when they take a stand. You've practiced giving generously and receiving graciously. You've practiced cultivating gratitude, giving your sacred gifts, and forming relationships of reciprocity where people share with each other over time.

You've practiced receiving the Earth's gifts with gratitude, and giving back to the Earth. You've questioned your assumptions, practiced bravery, and channeled your anger in productive ways.

You've joined with other people into groups that continually share with each other, and where people can safely speak their heart. You've practiced holding yourself and others to high standards and making it easy for others to do the same for you.

If you haven't done all the activities, that's ok! They are life-long practices, meant to be done repeatedly so they become a way of life. If you haven't begun, that's ok too. Now is a good time to start.

Build a Healthy Community One Person at a Time

A great way to begin building a healthy community, and eventually a healthy nation, is to build the *most amazing friendships ever*.

What kind of friends do you want to have? Do you want friends who have your back no matter what, who share and support you and always tell the truth, who care about the Earth and enjoy life? If you want friends like that, what kind of friend would you need to be?

Of course – you'd need to be that kind of friend too.

Many people want friendships based on the golden rule. Whether you find them online, at shops, at political events, anarchist spaces, in your neighborhood, or by chance, they will be glad to meet you.

Find others who also want rich friendships, and practice the revolutionary activities together. When you make a good friend, practice supporting each other, sharing, standing for what's right, holding each other to a high standard, encouraging each person to give their sacred gifts, and cultivating bravery. Practice creating private spaces so you can speak freely.

Deep friendships usually take time to grow, but they will grow a lot faster if you have a clear intention for the kind of friendship you want to have, and the kind of friend you want to be. Speak openly with each other about the kind of relationship you want, and how you commit to showing up to make it happen. Listen to what the other person wants and what they are willing to commit to, and find your common ground. You don't need to agree to be revolutionaries; just focus on building a great friendship.

Some people don't believe in deep friendships. Others only look for "perfect" people who never make mistakes, so they're constantly disappointed. Everyone makes mistakes, even Jesus Christ and Harriet Tubman. Look for people willing to walk a special journey together, one where you consistently bring out the best in each other and help each other acknowledge and grow from mistakes.

Many people have little time and energy to develop deep friendships due to all kinds of stressors, such as keeping their job, rearing children, and worrying about politics. Find ways to share your time and energy so that overworked parents can have some time away from kids without resorting to electronic "babysitters," or so people can feel resilient if their job goes away. If someone lives in a food desert, help them get fresh produce. If someone can't afford fresh produce, help them find a worktrade opportunity so they don't need to pay to eat well.

Have fun together. Go on camping trips and share stories around the fire, make music in someone's living room, and celebrate milestones in kids' lives, like their first step or first successful hunt.

Build up each other's dignity. Train self-defense and bravery together. Help each other remember what's important in life – taking care of each other and the Earth. Being around people with high standards is a great antidote for the superficiality on TV.

Build spiritual strength together, with each person bringing out the best in everyone else. When you help each other and the Earth, living with high standards for yourself and each other, you will become more than a group of friends. You will become a healthy community, choosing your own beautiful way of life together despite the laws and pressures of your unhealthy nation.

This is the difference between a friend group or collection of neighbors and a healthy community. Friends and neighbors may enjoy each other's company, but they may not have the same values and usually don't have their own high standards of behavior for each other. In healthy communities, whether people live nearby or more spread out, people do share many of the same values and, crucially, they hold themselves and each other to high standards.

Most people struggle to hold each other to high standards for a variety of reasons. Some people demand obedience and impose their personal will, just as obedience was expected of them in childhood. Others reject shared standards that are clearly defined and firmly upheld, thinking that any imposition on an individual is an authoritarian restriction of autonomy, and after all who are they to say what's right and wrong? Both attitudes lead to poor boundaries and low standards, leading to different kinds of hurtful behavior that will undermine any community.

Holding yourself and others to a high standard and expecting others to do the same isn't about one person imposing on another. When everyone agrees on their rules or standards of good behavior, no one imposes anything on anyone else. A misbehaving person is merely reminded of their commitment to the high standards, and asked to live up to them.

Taking a stand when someone misbehaves is often not "nice" or comfortable. You must cultivate bravery so you can uphold your community's standards even when it's uncomfortable. With bravery, you can show a misbehaving person the mistake they're making, invite them to show up better, and hold a clear, healthy boundary if they choose not to change.

High standards are not optional. You will not have a healthy community of deep trust without high standards. Many people have tried to form intentional communities and found them dissatisfying, and often they transform into mere groups of neighbors as trust diminishes over time. Why?

Healthy communities are based on trust, and there are many ways people want to trust each other – trust that others will tell the truth, keep their promises, act in service, and stand for justice as needed (integrity). Trust that others will do the right thing even if it's scary or uncomfortable (bravery). Trust that people will share and care for each other (kindness and generosity). Trust that others will see and understand them (awareness). Trust that people will protect each other as needed (bravery and selfless violence). Trust that people will take accountability for their mistakes, and forgive others when they take accountability (accountability and compassion). Ultimately, we want to trust people to live by the golden rule – to treat others as we would want to be treated.

If your community doesn't hold people to high standards in all these areas, deep trust will not grow, and it will be a group of friendly neighbors at best. To keep a community healthy, you must confront inappropriate behavior, either supporting someone in their spiritual growth or asking them to leave if they refuse to grow.

Recognize which differences you can tolerate and which you cannot. Differences in things like clothing, language, skin color, and sexuality can all be tolerated or even celebrated in a healthy community. What cannot be tolerated are the hurtful qualities described here, including low integrity, cowardice, and selfishness.

Many people who say they want community focus on minimizing conflict, even if it means telling "little" lies or pretending to ignore when someone breaks a promise. In effect, this just means tolerating inappropriate behavior, and distrust becomes normal.

Recall the Haudenosaunee writers' words: "if absolute justice was established in the world, peace would naturally follow."[207]

Peace in a community doesn't come because people avoid conflict. Peace comes when everyone stands for what's right, confronting inappropriate behavior as needed to hold each other to high standards. When you do this, peace and trust will naturally follow.

Do not rely on artificial intelligence chatbots (AI) to make your decisions or give you "advice." Every AI transcript is recorded and available to any corporation or agency that wants it. Chatbots are very manipulative, often saying what they "think" the user wants to hear, not what would aid their spiritual growth. There is no substitute for you developing the spiritual strength to stand for what's right as needed. Consult with trusted friends when you need support. If you don't have trusted friends yet, go find them. They will be glad to meet you.

You also cannot rely on any particular system of self-governance to keep your community healthy. Whether you use consensus, democracy, sociocracy, or anything else, no system of government will maintain a baseline of mutual respect if people lack spiritual strength. If that spiritual strength is strong and widespread, many forms of self-governance can work. This explains why, among the Haudenosaunee, "many of the rules… are designed to create a strong society rather than a strong government."[208]

As a healthy community of people with high expectations, your group's standards of appropriate behavior will become the laws you live by – laws based not on dominance, exploitation and selfishness but on justice, generosity, integrity, kindness, and bravery.

The Haudenosaunee writers described how their "society was founded on concepts of moral justice, not statute law."[207] Such a society can only exist when everyone has that spiritual strength to stand for what's right. And building new healthy communities where people joyfully cultivate that spiritual strength together is part of the path to building a new healthy nation.

Revolutionary Activity #35
Talk clearly about the kind of friendship you want

Think about what kind of friendships you want. Approach someone with whom you want a strong friendship, and ask if they'd like to discuss the sort of relationship you two could have. Tell them clearly what you want, such as a friendship where each person can rely on the other to tell the truth, to share, and protect and support each other in hard times. Tell them that you're willing to commit to these things – whatever qualities you choose – to make this friendship real. Ask them what they want in the friendship and what they will commit to. Find common ground, so you're both excited about the quality of friendship you're committing to have with each other.

> When you set clear, high standards and meet them, and help each other grow from mistakes, this creates deep trust faster than just "letting the relationship happen."

Build Spiritual Strength with Others

Many people don't learn to hold good boundaries in their personal life. Often people tolerate inappropriate behavior towards themselves, or act hurtfully towards others.

This is because people in unhealthy nations are not allowed to set the boundaries they live by. Laws are imposed on them which they're not allowed to uphold, meaning most people live within boundaries that others choose and enforce. Much of the spiritual growth required to live in a healthy community involves learning how to hold good boundaries.

Selfishness may seem normal, but it is a poison for healthy communities which must hold good boundaries to keep it out.

Many people are not ready to live in healthy communities. Some people won't see the value in them. Infiltrators pretend to want community but actually try to sabotage it. Others want community but aren't really committed to the depth of spiritual growth needed to show up in a good way. These people need to be prevented from joining the community, or evicted if they are allowed in, at least until they change their ways.

Other people truly want to live in a healthy community, but they've learned bad habits and sometimes they act hurtfully. But they are committed to growing, and when they are approached respectfully they change their ways and show up better.

Some of the deepest work of building healthy communities is learning when to forgive and when to hold good boundaries and evict someone whose continued misbehavior threatens the whole community's honest and generous way of life.

If you let anyone participate and don't hold boundaries, selfish people will push out the generous ones, dishonest people will push out the honest ones, and trust will dissipate. This is common.

Also, if you commonly evict someone for any thoughtless act or momentary selfishness, then people will feel vulnerable and afraid to make mistakes and the community still won't last.

It must be ok to make a mistake and trust that people know you're willing to learn and make amends. At the same time it is important to have high standards of behavior that everybody is continuously striving to meet, and if someone isn't actually committed to those high standards, they must leave for the good of the community.

As you build your community, you will encounter people who lie or break a promise, and you must choose whether to trust them again. A crucial question to answer is this: "Is the person clearly committed to spiritual growth so that, if they are shown their hurtful behavior and how to show up better, they will grow from it and not make the same mistake again?"

If someone makes a mistake and you respectfully confront them, what happens? If they make excuses or attack you, then hold a strong boundary and refuse to trust them. If they acknowledge their mistake, apologize, make up for any harm done, and truly commit to doing better, then you may find that you're willing to trust them, perhaps even more than before. When counseling goes well, both people cultivate a deeper awareness and integrity, and it builds mutual trust that you can work through troubles when they arise.

"Perfect" has a few meanings. In one sense, everyone is perfect because everyone is basically good. In another sense, no one is perfect because everyone makes mistakes. Many people have developed bad habits and subconscious hurtful behaviors. Expect people, including yourself, to make mistakes and act hurtfully, often without knowing it. Be ready for these challenges.

A person doesn't need to be "perfect" or never make mistakes in order to be trustworthy. The willingness to take accountability for mistakes and grow from them lets a person cultivate deep integrity and become very trustworthy.

Likewise, no relationship is perfect, but relationships can *deepen* when people commit to growing together over time.

Since everyone will make mistakes at times, every healthy community needs a *path back to grace*. This is a process where the community recognizes when someone has grown from their mistake and returns to trusting them again.

People cannot be afraid that any slip-up will cause them to be kicked out. There has to be a path back to grace so that people who act hurtfully or violate people's trust can return to being trusted again if they show that they are truly committed to high standards for themselves and others.

A person may lie or act selfishly because they don't trust others to handle the truth gracefully, or to remain friends after admitting their mistake. Counseling can also be a chance for the community to reflect on ways they unknowingly discourage good behavior.

The essential attitude for holding good boundaries is this: *everyone is basically good, but some attitudes and behaviors such as cowardice or dishonesty are toxic to a healthy community and must not be allowed to stay.* For the good of the community, these hurtful attitudes or behaviors must go. Either a person can grow, or they must leave and take their hurtful attitudes and behaviors with them. Either way, the community maintains its high standards.

Learning when to forgive and how to hold good boundaries may sound hard, but it is part of the art of being human, and in a healthy community no single person makes these decisions alone.

Even the Zapatistas make mistakes. Major Moisés described their self-governance changes and he said that "we are just learning and… it will take a while to get going well."[199]

This is why it's important to build spiritual strength together. Making and upholding your own laws (i.e. holding people to a high standard of behavior) is a big responsibility.

So commit to that path of deep spiritual growth with others. Expect that mistakes will happen, and learn to grow and forgive. And when necessary, learn to hold healthy boundaries too so that, one way or another, selfishness will not take hold in your community.

> **Revolutionary Activity #36**
> **What does your path back to grace look like?**
> Think of someone who disappointed you recently. Perhaps they lied to you or didn't keep a promise. Decide what words you would need to hear from them, and what actions you would need to see for you to begin trusting them again. Ensure your path back to grace follows the golden rule, so you treat others the way you would want to be treated.

If the Zapatistas Can Do It, So Can We

Building a healthy nation is challenging. Unhealthy nations encourage superficiality, ineffective political movements, division, deceit, and selfishness. Many people learn to feel helpless or not care about anything, as their society seems so sick and there's no clear path of deep change.

It would be hard enough to grow up surrounded by these hurtful qualities and then embrace a way of life based on integrity, generosity, and connection instead. It becomes immensely harder when authorities sabotage solidarity, train people for obedience, spread lies, murder spiritual leaders, abuse children, and keep people in poverty.

The Zapatistas showed that the path to freedom may be difficult and dangerous, yet every one of them chose to walk it so they could escape this terrible way of life and create a healthy nation instead. And each of us can walk a similar path.

With strong relationships and steady spiritual strength, you and your friends will be ready to address difficult questions, including how to build or acquire the needed weapons for self-defense and how to organize the communities so that the nation can protect itself. The Zapatistas offer helpful details in their writings.[12]

Just like the Zapatistas, every person in every unhealthy nation today has ancestors who once lived in healthy nations sometime in the past. For some it was only years or decades ago. For many others it's been centuries or millennia. Those ancestors enjoyed a way of life based on the three core spiritual practices, where every moment and every relationship was meaningful, life was full of joyful gratitude, and people gave their deepest love as a normal way of life without holding back.

At some point, our ancestors suffered something terrible, and eventually the unhealthy nation started to seem "just the way life is." But despite all the oppression, this truth remains: being treated with care and respect, feeding others and being fed, meeting life's needs with meaningful work, and living closely with strong and caring people feels wonderful. And it feels so incredibly wonderful because *this is who we really are*.

Each one of us has the same urges towards gratitude, integrity, sharing, and all the other beautiful qualities described in this book, even if some people have learned to ignore those urges in order to survive in their unhealthy nation. It's our human nature to live in healthy nations embracing these qualities. "Human nature" describes how humans live when we can choose how to live, not how people behave when they're abused, threatened, chronically insecure, isolated, and unable to live in a deeply satisfying way.

So spread the good news! You could potentially live in a nation that maintains a respectful way of life among the people, and between the people and the Earth. Cultivate your spiritual strength, and build deep relationships with other people and the Earth.

Someday you may live in a free nation, or perhaps you will lay the groundwork so that a future generation can. Even if you're just good to the Earth and the people around you right now, no matter what else happens, it will be worth it.

Revolutionary Activity #37
Join a group dedicated to spiritual growth

Join or found a men's group or women's group dedicated to each person's spiritual growth. Meet regularly and help each other work through daily challenges with beautiful qualities such as integrity, kindness, generosity, bravery, and awareness. Support each other to cultivate and give your sacred gifts. If everyone in the group struggles in the same way, such as having low integrity, take care to truly have high standards and not reinforce each others' weaknesses.

Chapter 18: The Deepest Revolution

Your unhealthy nation might seem impossibly stuck with big troubles like racism, sexism, poverty, corruption, pollution, and child abuse. So many challenges to solve!

But all these different issues stem from one root problem: *we are not free*. We can neither choose our laws nor enforce them. Instead, we must obey laws imposed on us, and we are punished for standing for what's right and directly seeking justice. As long as we are not free, all the other issues will persist.

Troubles like corruption, greed and discrimination are merely *symptoms* of a *root cultural disease* where a few people rule, and the rest accept their own submissive obedience as legitimate. As every doctor knows, treating symptoms will never lead to deep healing while the underlying disease persists.

Any political movement that ignores this root disease is only asking their rulers to please be nicer, or please follow the laws they impose on others. There has never been a system of constitutional "checks and balances" that causes rulers to obey their own laws, or makes justice universal. No anti-racism movement in human history has ever ended racism in their unhealthy nation, and no anti-sexism movement has ended sexism. As long as a person or group rules your nation, these troubles will continue.

But there is a cure to this cultural disease and all its symptoms: create a new healthy nation where everybody agrees on their laws and takes personal responsibility to uphold them, taking the people's and Earth's needs into account. Some people will not want to walk this path, but many will.

This path starts with you. Learn to hold yourself to a high standard of integrity, generosity, and all the other beautiful qualities in this book. Make amazing friendships with others who are also committed to creating a respectful way of life, and form healthy communities where each person holds themselves and others to a high standard of excellent behavior, collectively creating your own law based on kindness, integrity, respect for the Earth, and pervasive justice.

Then join with other healthy communities to eventually form a new healthy nation, where each community protects the others so that this new nation can endure even while surrounded by unhealthy nations with their endless troubles.

Whether or not you're able to create a new nation, each step of this journey by itself will be transformative and worth the effort.

We Are the Promised Land

Some people say the arc of history bends towards justice. I say the arc of history bends whichever way people bend it.

Ultimately, we remain in an abusive nation because we tolerate it. Yes, there has been a massive amount of shame, violence, broken promises, lies, and spiritual wounding that make deep change really hard. Rulers and their servants use so many tricks and traps to get us to tolerate our own abuse and accept our submissiveness as legitimate and "just the way life is."

The only way to end this abuse is to stand up for ourselves. That's the Deepest Revolution: when enough people stand together and take care of each other even at great personal risk in order to create a different way of life. The arc of history bends when enough people give their divine love fully, right now, rather than holding back, hoping to avoid abuse for another day.

The night before his murder, Martin Luther King Jr said, "I've seen the promised land. I may not get there with you. But I want you to know tonight, that we, as a people, will get to the promised land."[138]

I'm telling you I've BEEN to the promised land. I've lived with a whole healthy nation where people routinely have integrity, generosity, respect for men, women and children, deep connection with the Earth, strong leaders, and no rulers.

The promised land is real, and I'll tell you what else I learned – *WE are the promised land*. Every single person can be one of our many messiahs, one of our many liberators as we free ourselves from the biggest trap in human history. And the more messiahs, the more liberators, the better. We are our own saviors.

The path won't be easy, as Jesus Christ, Harriet Tubman, and other spiritual leaders around the world have shown. But now is the time. People are suffering as prison slaves. Pollution is causing all manner of diseases and destruction. Racism and sexism persist, as do wars that kill the poor and profit the rich. Nonhumans are suffering and dying in large numbers, and humans won't last long if we don't change course.

Kings and billionaires of unhealthy nations threaten, bribe, trick, and trap people to support so many terrible things. To free ourselves, we must create new healthy nations, one community at a time, where people live with mutual respect for each other and the Earth.

So cultivate your spiritual strength and support others in cultivating theirs. Stand for what's right together, protecting each other and the Earth. And I promise you will not stand alone.

Millions of people are standing for the Earth and standing for cultures of mutual respect right now. Many of us were born into healthy nations, and many of us were not. In countless different ways, all around the world, we are taking this stand together.

And I'd love for you to join us.

* * *

For future updates, opportunities, and connections, sign up here:
https://thedeepestrevolution.com/signup

Glossary

Following are key terms and the chapters where they are discussed.

Assumptions: Unexamined beliefs. (11)

Bravery: The ability to remain conscious of what you know is right and act in service even if you feel uncomfortable or afraid. (4, 9, 13, 14, 17)

Cowardice: Prioritizing one's comfort over standing for what's right, the opposite of bravery. Training children for obedience trains them for cowardice, as they learn to protect their comfort by obeying rather than bravely do what's right. (13, 14, 17)

Freedom: A way of life where everyone in a nation expects themselves and everyone else to stand for what's right. Everyone agrees on their laws and bravely upholds them so justice, protection, and mutual respect are normal. (5, 7, 9, 13, 15, 17)

Healthy community: Communities where people hold each other to high standards of behavior, including generosity, integrity, and deep connection with the Earth so that trust and mutual aid are common. Healthy communities are the building blocks of healthy nations. (5, 8, 10, 17)

Integrity: The willingness to stand for a culture of mutual respect, including being honest, keeping promises, having an attitude of service, and standing for justice. (2, 5, 6, 7, 13, 14, 17)

Laws: Widely recognized standards of appropriate or inappropriate behavior in a nation or community. (5, 17)

Nation: A group of people with laws and clear ways of responding to internal misbehavior or external threats. Communities within a nation protect each other from outside attack. (5)

Nation, healthy: A nation where the people agree on their laws and everyone is expected to bravely uphold them as a normal way of life so that justice and mutual respect are normal. Qualities like generosity, integrity, and connection with the Earth are widespread, so trust is widespread too. (Every chapter)

Nation, unhealthy: A nation where a ruling class imposes laws and expects submissive obedience from everyone else. Troubles like corruption, greed, discrimination, and child abuse become normalized and rampant, as do personal qualities like cowardice and superficiality. (1, 5-14)

Reciprocity: A way of life where gifts are never "paid back" and humans and nonhumans keep giving to each other, deepening mutual gratitude over time. (7, 17)

Spirituality: How a person relates to themselves and the world. (3, 8, 13, 16)

Spiritual leader: Someone who helps people relate to themselves and the world in a good way, including with awareness, integrity, generosity, bravery, and solidarity with others. Spiritual leaders help their people confront troubles like injustice, poverty, low self-worth, and disconnection from the Earth. (2, 8, 9, 16)

Spiritual strength: The ability to give one's deepest love and stand for what's right in service of others. (5, 6, 8, 9, 14, 16, 17)

Selfless violence: Violence in service of others, especially defending one's community or nation from attack. (12, 17)

Selfish violence: When a person commits violence or orders others to commit violence for the individual's benefit at the expense of the nation. Examples include authorities punishing peace activists who oppose unjust wars and killing spiritual leaders who confront injustices. (8, 9, 10, 12)

Slavery: A way of life where people follow laws they don't choose and often don't like, knowingly obey corrupt leaders, and believe that this is ok. Submissive obedience, selfishness, superficiality, and cowardice are common while integrity is rare. (9)

The three core spiritual practices: The spiritual foundation for living in healthy communities and healthy nations: cultivating a practical, aware gratitude for the gifts of life; giving one's sacred gifts; and living in reciprocity with people and the Earth. (3, 16)

Locations of Healthy Nations Referenced in this Book

Africa

Akamba	Mbuti	San

Asia

Evenk	Jenu Kuruba	Mongol	Mosuo
Nivkh			

Australia

Gumbaynggirr

Europe

Sami

North America

Apache	Cherokee	Cheyenne	Cree
Crow	Eskimo	Haudenosaunee	Huron
Lakota	Mohawk	Montagnais-Naskapi	Nez Perce
Nootka	Okanagan	Potawatomi	Sioux
Tzutujil Maya	Zapatista		

South America

Ashaninka	Kulina	Tchimane	Yequana
Yuracare			

Important Notes on Sensitive Topics

Capitalization of People's Titles

I chose not to capitalize anybody's title in this book, including president, chief, king, or minister. Healthy nations maintain a baseline of mutual respect internally, and they consistently describe the importance of keeping everyone on the same level. For example, the San remind their hunters of how much they depend on their neighbors, and not to feel superior.[187] Tzutujil Mayans expected new chiefs to give away all their things so everyone was on the same economic level.[219]

Making titles lowercase reminded me that no one's title makes them special. And people without titles are no less worthy of respect.

On Sharing Others' Stories

If someone published their stories in a book available to the public, I chose to include some of the stories here with attribution and a respectful retelling. Whenever I privately received a story or perspective about healthy nations, I asked permission to share and got feedback to ensure it was presented as intended.

I did my best to quote or summarize all stories and cultural practices correctly, and distinguish between my own beliefs and those of others. I accept responsibility for any mistakes or misinterpretations I may have made.

On Healthy Nations' Names

This book uses widely recognized English names of healthy nations to make it accessible to a wide audience, and with that limitation, it uses the names that authors or speakers used to refer to themselves. For example, Ohiyesa commonly referred to himself and his people as the Sioux in his books, while Black Elk referred to his people as the Lakota. Thus when this book references stories or quotes from Ohiyesa the book refers to the Sioux, and when the book cites Black Elk it refers to the Lakota.

On Healthy Nations Past and Present

In order to contrast healthy and unhealthy nations, I sought out stories from when each healthy nation could fully embrace their traditional practices and way of life. Many healthy nations have been unable to live in a traditional way since unhealthy nations imposed their laws and various forms of oppression.

Okanagan Jeannette Armstrong described this when she said, "I'm not saying that [the traditional Okanagan decision-making process is] there today, that it works today, but elements of it are still present and have been carried forward because we are only two generations since colonization began."[183]

This book refers to many traditional practices that were fully observed in the past and uses the past tense to describe these, especially when a speaker like Pretty Shield (Crow) or Black Elk (Lakota) spoke about them in the past tense. However, these nations continue to exist and embrace attitudes and practices from which others can learn a great deal.

Acknowledging Contradictions

This book makes the case that healthy nations are able to maintain a basically respectful way of life. However, I did find seeming contradictions in my research. For example, Prechtel described how the Tzutujil Mayans had "lords" and "ladies",[217] a Nootka storyteller referenced royalty and slavery,[36] and American John Adams described a Haudenosaunee "king" and "nobles."[176]

Seeming contradictions can occur for many reasons. Often they are a simple misunderstanding: John Adams assumed every nation had rulers so he assumed the Haudenosaunee did too, but he was wrong. Sometimes words mean different things to different people, and clearly Tzutujil Mayan lords and ladies didn't have wealth or power over others the way they do in European countries.[219] Also, not every North or South American nation was healthy prior to Europeans' arrival. It takes judgment to choose which lessons to learn from which nations in which time period. The book *One Disease One Cure* offers a more in-depth review of contradictions.

Copyright, Image Credits & Further Reading

This book is copyrighted by William Randolph in 2025 under the Creative Commons CC BY-NC-ND 4.0 license. Readers may copy and redistribute the material in any medium or format. To view a copy of this license, visit https://creativecommons.org/licenses/by-nc-nd/4.0/

If you want to use material from this book in a way not supported by the license, please contact me through the book's website: https://thedeepestrevolution.com/contact/

Nothing in this book is intended to substitute for personalized advice from trusted practitioners in health, law, or any field. The author accepts no liability for any results of reading this book.

ISBNs: 979-8-9920652-3-7 (Digital); 979-8-9920652-2-0 (Print)

Image Credits: Cover: *Sophia Mueller;* Chapter 3: "Hawks Hunting": *Chelsea Spitzer;* Chapter 6: "Riot Police in Venezuela": *AP Photo/Ariana Cubillos,*[52] "Riot Police in China": *AP Photo/Eugene Hoshiko,*[104] "Riot Police in the United States": *Graeme Sloan/Sipa USA;*[249] Chapter 8: "Sabotaging Efforts at Deep Cultural Healing": *Chelsea Spitzer;* Chapter 10: "When People Fall for Scams like Racism": *Chelsea Spitzer.* Reproduced with permission.

Further Reading: One Disease One Cure offers a more comprehensive, detailed exploration of healthy and unhealthy nations. It includes many themes which were not included in *The Deepest Revolution,* including sexuality, privilege, entitlement, stories of creating healthy communities (called "healthy subcultures" in that book), nutrition, ancient religious misunderstandings, and much more.

Both *The Deepest Revolution* and *One Disease One Cure* are free to download and have a physical version available. Both books are available at http://thedeepestrevolution.com. All profits will be donated to protect people and the Earth from exploitation.

Bibliography

1. 10 Microaggressions Companies Must Avoid. (2024, August 4). SHRM. https://www.shrm.org/topics-tools/news/inclusion-diversity/10-microaggressions-to-avoid
2. 2018-11-21 Central University of Venezuela. (2018, November 21). Scholars at Risk. https://www.scholarsatrisk.org/report/2018-11-21-central-university-of-venezuela/
3. 2021 Tax Form 990-PF Chan Zuckerberg Initiative Foundation. (2024). Chan Zuckerberg Initiative Foundation. https://projects.propublica.org/nonprofits/organizations/455002209/202233199349108343/full
4. 2021 Tax Form 990-PF for Omidyar Network Fund, Inc. (n.d.). Omidyar Network Fund, Inc. https://omidyar.com/wp-content/uploads/2022/12/2021-ONFI-Fed-990-PF_PUBLIC.pdf
5. About Us. (2024, August 4). M4BL. https://m4bl.org/about-us/
6. Abramson, J., & Acosta, A. (2023, April 27). As War Leads to More Orders, Weapons Makers Should Embrace Human Rights. Investor Advocates for Social Justice. https://iasj.org/as-war-leads-to-more-orders-weapons-makers-should-embrace-human-rights/
7. Ahmadi, A. (2025, March 8). Trump pulls $400 million from Columbia University over Gaza protests. BBC. https://www.bbc.com/news/articles/c4gp979w055o
8. AJLabs. (2025, April 17). Israel-Gaza war in maps and charts: Live tracker. Al Jazeera. https://www.aljazeera.com/news/longform/2023/10/9/israel-hamas-war-in-maps-and-charts-live-tracker

Allen, P. (1991). Grandmothers of the Light. Beacon Press.

9. p. 9

10. Anderson, K. (1985). Commodity Exchange and Subordination: Montagnais-Naskapi and Huron Women, 1600-1650. Chicago Journals, 11(1), 48–62.
11. Arbuthnot, Mollie. (2019, August 27). World Revolution / Postcolonial Paradise: Utopian Visions of the 'Soviet East' in the 1920-30s. The Language of 'Authoritarian' Regimes. https://thelanguageofauthoritarianregimes.wordpress.com/2019/08/27/world-revolution-postcolonial-paradise-utopian-visions-of-the-soviet-east-in-the-1920-30s/
12. Archivo Histórico. (2025, September 7). Enlace Zapatista. https://enlacezapatista.ezln.org.mx/category/1994/
13. Arnold, D. G., Stewart, O. J., & Beck, T. (2020). Financial Penalties Imposed on Large Pharmaceutical Firms for Illegal Activities. JAMA, 324(19), 1995–1997. https://doi.org/10.1001/jama.2020.18740
14. Assange, J. (2007, January 3). Selected Correspondence. IQ.Org. https://web.archive.org/web/20070110200827/http://iq.org/
15. Auble, D. (2021). Capitalizing on Conflict: How defense contractors and foreign nations lobby for arms sales. Open Secrets. https://www.opensecrets.org/news/reports/capitalizing-on-conflict/defense-contractors
16. Bailey, S. (1957). 'Police Socialism' in Tsarist Russia. The Review of Politics, 19(4), 462–471.

Ballantine, B., & Ballantine, I. (Eds.). (2001). The Native Americans An Illustrated History. Turner Publishing.

17. p. 156

Baptist, E. (2014). The Half Has Never Been Told. Basic Books.

18. Chapter "1805-1861"
19. Bargallie, D. (2023). Indigenous Australian Peoples and Work: Examining Worklife Histories. In S. Billett, H. Salling Olesen, & L. Filliettaz (Eds.), Sustaining Employability Through Work-life Learning: Practices and Policies (pp. 127–144). Springer Nature. https://doi.org/10.1007/978-981-99-3959-6_6

Barrett, S. (2010). Geronimo's Story of His Life. Project Gutenberg.

20. Chapter "Introductory"
21. Chapter "KAS-KI-YEH"
22. Chapter "Preparation of a Warrior"
23. Chapter "The Family"
24. Chapter "Unwritten Laws of the Apaches"
25. Basket, N. (2023, August 5). Nancy Basket Interview [Personal communication].
26. Baum, D. (2016, April). Legalize It All. Harper's Magazine, April 2016. https://harpers.org/archive/2016/04/legalize-it-all/
27. Bettelheim, B. (1943). Individual and Mass Behavior in Extreme Situations. Journal of Abnormal and Social Psychology, XXXVIII(4), 417–452. https://doi.org/10.1037/h0061208
28. Binswanger, I. A., Stern, M. F., & Et al. (2007). Release from Prison-A High Risk of Death for Former Inmates. New England Journal of Medicine, 356(2), 157–165. https://doi.org/10.1056/NEJMsa064115
29. Blumberg, N. (2025, August 3). The Star-Spangled Banner | USA, National Anthem, Lyrics, Song, & Meaning | Britannica. Encyclopedia Britannica. https://www.britannica.com/topic/The-Star-Spangled-Banner
30. Boissoneault, L. (2017, February 21). The True Story of the Reichstag Fire and the Nazi Rise to Power. Smithsonian Magazine. https://www.smithsonianmag.com/history/true-story-reichstag-fire-and-nazis-rise-power-180962240/
31. Bradford, S. (2020). Harriet, the Moses of Her People. Project Gutenberg. https://www.gutenberg.org/ebooks/9999

Brown Jr, T. (2003). The Vision. One Spirit.

32. p. 126   **33.** p. 81

Cameron, A. (1981). Daughters of Copper Woman. Press Gang Publishers.

34. pp. 101-102   **35.** pp. 109-112   **36.** p. 11
37. p. 112   **38.** p. 62   **39.** p. 71
40. pp. 73-74   **41.** p. 79

42. Cartwright, S. (1851). Report on the Diseases and Physical Peculiarities of the Negro Race. New Orleans Medical and Surgical Journal, 691–715.

Catechism of the Catholic Church. (1997). Doubleday.

43. p. 405   **44.** p. 408   **45.** pp. 416-418

46. Churchill, W. (1947, November 11). The Worst Form of Government. International Churchill Society. https://winstonchurchill.org/resources/quotes/the-worst-form-of-government/

47. Conkar, Z. (2024, October 7). TRT Global-Repression and resistance: How Germany is stifling pro-Palestinian voie. TRT Global. https://trt.global/world/article/18216880

48. Cook, J. (2020, September 2). For years, journalists cheered Assange's abuse. Now they've paved his path to a US gulag. Jonathan Cook Blog. https://www.jonathan-cook.net/blog/2020-09-02/media-assange-persecution/

49. Copp, T. (2023, October 13). Here's what military assistance the US is providing Israel since Hamas assault. The Times of Israel. https://www.timesofisrael.com/heres-what-military-assistance-the-us-is-providing-israel-since-hamas-assault/

Cox, D. (2019). Just Another Nigger. Heyday.

50. Chapter "Just Another Nigger"   **51.** Chapter "Use What You Got to Get What You Need"

52. Cubillos, A. (2018, November 21). Venezuela Student Protest. Associated Press. https://newsroom.ap.org/editorial-photos-videos/detail?itemid=4216e2db097e4a4384950ed63e068a37&mediatype=photo

Daly, J. (2004). The Watchful State. Northern Illinois University Press.

53. pp. 8-12

54. Debunking the idea of Protected Areas. (2023, March 22). Community Networks Against Protected Areas. https://assets.survivalinternational.org/documents/2471/CNAPA_Concept_Note.docx

DeCamp, J. (1996). The Franklin Cover-Up.

55. pp. 4-12   **56.** p. xvii

57. Deforestation and Forest Degradation: The Causes, Effects, and Solutions. (2025, April 9). NRDC. https://www.nrdc.org/stories/deforestation-forest-degradation-causes-effects-solutions

58. Denova, R. (2022, February 10). Zealots. World History Encyclopedia. https://www.worldhistory.org/Zealots

59. Director of Central Intelligence, Assistant Director, Research and Reports. (1951, April 2). Suggestions on the kinds of projects we would like to see the Ford Foundation Support. CIA. https://www.cia.gov/readingroom/docs/CIA-RDP79-01157A000100060036-2.pdf

60. Dismantle Israel's carceral regime and 'open-air' imprisonment of Palestinians: UN expert. (2023, July 10). OHCHR. https://www.ohchr.org/en/press-releases/2023/07/dismantle-israels-carceral-regime-and-open-air-imprisonment-palestinians-un

61. Douglass, J. (2000, Spring). Martin Luther King Assassination Conspiracy Exposed in Memphis. Ratical.Org. https://ratical.org/ratville/JFK/Unspeakable/MLKconExp.html

62. Dunbar, R. (2021, August 28). Dunbar's Number: Why the Theory That Humans Can Only Maintain 150 Friendships Has Withstood 30 Years of Scrutiny. Neuroscience News. https://neurosciencenews.com/dunbars-number-social-brain-19210/

Eastman (Ohiyesa), C. A. (1916). From the Deep Woods to Civilization. Little, Brown, and Company.

63. Chapter "Civilization as Preached and Practiced"   **64.** Chapter "College Life in the East"   **65.** Chapter "On the White Man's Trail"
66. Chapter "The Way Opens"

Eastman (Ohiyesa), C. A. (2008). Indian Child Life. Project Gutenberg.

67. Chapter "Early Hardships"   **68.** Chapter "The Faithfulness of Long Ears"

Eastman (Ohiyesa), C. A. (2013). Indian Heroes and Great Chieftains. Project Gutenberg.

69. Chapter "Chief Joseph"   **70.** Chapter "Crazy Horse"   **71.** Chapter "Sitting Bull"

72. Edwards, R. (2006). White Death: Russia's War With Finland 1939-40. Weidenfeld & Nicolson.

English Standard Version Bible. (n.d.).

73. John 6:38   **74.** Mark 11:15-18   **75.** Mark 2:23-24
76. Matthew 12:10   **77.** Matthew 27:12

78. Evans, R., & Lewis, P. (2012, January 20). Undercover police had children with activists. The Guardian. https://www.theguardian.com/uk/2012/jan/20/undercover-police-children-activists

79. Everyday heroism makes the sparkles possible (Google Translate, Trans.). (1994, January 26). Enlace Zapatista. https://enlacezapatista.ezln.org.mx/1994/01/26/heroismo-cotidiano-hace-posible-que-existan-los-destellos/

80. Everyone Blames Me. (2017). Human Rights Watch. https://www.hrw.org/sites/default/files/report_pdf/india1117_web.pdf

81. Explosive Features | Twin Towers. (2024, August 4). AE911Truth. https://www.ae911truth.org/evidence/explosive-features

82. FBI releases declassified documents about investigating ties between Saudi government and Sept. 11 attacks. (2021, November 4). CBS News. https://www.cbsnews.com/news/fbi-declassified-documents-september-11-saudi-government/

83. FBI releases newly declassified record on September 11 attacks. (2021, September 12). Al Jazeera. https://www.aljazeera.com/news/2021/9/12/fbi-releases-newly-declassified-record-on-september-11-attacks

84. First Declaration of the Lacandon Jungle (Google Translate, Trans.). (1994, January 1). Enlace Zapatista. https://enlacezapatista.ezln.org.mx/1994/01/01/primera-declaracion-de-la-selva-lacandona/

85. Ford Foundation Announces $180 Million in New Funding for U.S. Racial Justice Efforts. (2020, October 9). Ford Foundation. https://www.fordfoundation.org/news-and-stories/news-and-press/news/ford-foundation-announces-180-million-in-new-funding-for-u-s-racial-justice-efforts/

86. Gaster, T., & Dimitrovsky, H. (2024, July 1). Judaism-Roman Period, 63 BCE-135 CE. Encyclopedia Britannica. https://www.britannica.com/topic/Judaism/The-Roman-period-63-bce-135-ce

87. Gauthier, M., & Pravettoni, R. (2016, August 30). Clashing over conservation: Saving Congo's forest and its Pygmies. The Guardian. https://www.theguardian.com/global-development/2016/aug/30/clashing-conservation-saving-democratic-republic-congo-forest-pygmies-drc

Gelder, S., & Gelder, R. (1964). The Timely Rain. Hutchinson.

88. p. 127

89. General Secretariat Organization of American States. (2007). Access to justice for women victims of violence in the Americas (No. OEA/Ser.L/V/II. Doc. 68). Organization of American States. https://www.ohchr.org/sites/default/files/lib-docs/HRBodies/UPR/Documents/session9/US/IACHR_Inter-AmericanCommission_Annex11.pdf

90. German police crack down on Palestinian activists in Berlin. (2022, May 17). New Arab. https://www.newarab.com/news/german-police-crack-down-palestinian-activists-berlin

91. Gibson, M. (Director). (2025a, July 14). Braveheart (1995)-Quotes-IMDb [Video recording]. https://www.imdb.com/title/tt0112573/quotes/

92. Gibson, M. (2025b, July 22). The Palestine Action crackdown. New Statesman. https://www.newstatesman.com/politics/2025/07/the-palestine-action-crackdown

93. Gilbert, G. (2024, July 17). Nuremberg Diary-by Gustave Gilbert Interview with Herman Goering. Mit.Edu. https://www.mit.edu/people/fuller/peace/war_goering.html

94. Goldstein, J. (2018, March 20). Promotions, Not Punishments, for Officers Accused of Lying. New York Times. https://www.nytimes.com/2018/03/19/nyregion/new-york-police-perjury-promotions.html

95. Government press office. (2023, October 11). Prime Minister Benjamin Netanyahu described the attacks as 'savagery… We have not seen since the Holocaust.' Barrons. https://www.barrons.com/video/prime-minister-benjamin-netanyahu-described-the-attacks-as-avagery-we-have-not-seen-since-the-holocaust/3D1FF6B4-E612-45A2-BC90-87BA79F875DD

Grinnell, G. (2005). When Buffalo Ran. Project Gutenberg.

96. Chapter "Lessons of the Prairie" 97. Chapter "The Attack on the Camp" 98. Chapter "The Way to Live"

99. 'Have you all lost your minds?'. Amazing and terrifying speech by @SWagenknecht. (2024, March 17). [Video recording]. https://rumble.com/v4jvdpu-have-you-all-lost-your-minds.-amazing-and-terrifying-speech-by-swagenknecht.html

100. Hertzgerg, M. (2021, November 28). Stasi Tactics – Zersetzung. Max Hertzberg. https://www.maxhertzberg.co.uk/background/politics/stasi-tactics/

Hingley, R. (2021). The Russian Secret Police. Routledge.

101. Chapter "The Okhrana in the Age of Assassinations 1901-1908"

102. Ho-de-no-sau-nee-ga (Haudenosaunee). (2024, July 2). Native Land Digital. https://native-land.ca/maps/territories/haudenosauneega-confederacy/

103. Hoover, J. E. (2024, August 4). The FBI Sets Goals for COINTELPRO. SHEC. https://shec.ashp.cuny.edu/items/show/814

104. Hoshiko, E. (2012, July 28). APTOPIX China Protest Plant. Associated Press. https://newsroom.ap.org/editorial-photos-videos/detail?itemid=2f230e39a6274de7aa94e6a5361be7cc&mediatype=photo

105. Impact. (2024, August 4). Black Lives Matter Impact Report. https://impact.blacklivesmatter.com/

106. Indigenous Clandestine Revolutionary Committee. (2005, June 20). On the Reasons for the General Red Alert (Google Translate, Trans.). EZLN. https://palabra.ezln.org.mx/comunicados/2005/2005_06_20_b.htm

107. Interview with Mayor Ana María: About the atrocities and the dirty war of the federal government (Google Translate, Trans.). (1995, February 13). Enlace Zapatista. https://enlacezapatista.ezln.org.mx/1995/02/13/entrevista-a-la-mayor-ana-maria-sobre-las-barbaridades-y-la-guerra-sucia-del-gobierno-federal/

108. Introduction-Ministry for State Security. (2024, August 4). Stasi-Unterlagen-Archiv. https://www.stasi-unterlagen-archiv.de/the-stasi/introduction/

109. Israel used 'calorie count' to limit Gaza food during blockade, critics claim. (2012, October 17). The Guardian. https://www.theguardian.com/world/2012/oct/17/israeli-military-calorie-limit-gaza

110. It Is Difficult to Get a Man to Understand Something When His Salary Depends Upon His Not Understanding It. (2017, November 30). Quote Investigator. https://quoteinvestigator.com/2017/11/30/salary/

Jackson, J. (2016). Black Elk The Life of an American Visionary. Farrar, Straus, and Giroux.

111. Chapter "Black Robe Days"

112. Chapter "Vanishing Americans"

113. Jenu Kuruba. (2024, August 24). Survival International. https://www.survivalinternational.org/tribes/jenu-kuruba

Johansen, B., & Mann, B. (2000). Encyclopedia of the Haudenosaunee. Greenwood Press.

114. p. 265

115. p. vii

116. Johnson, C. (2023, February 22). The vast majority of criminal cases end in plea bargains, a new report finds. NPR. https://www.npr.org/2023/02/22/1158356619/plea-bargains-criminal-cases-justicehttps://www.npr.org/2023/02/22/1158356619/plea-bargains-criminal-cases-justice

117. Johnstone, C. (2023, January 8). Caitlin Johnstone: Unprovoked! Consortium News. https://consortiumnews.com/2023/01/08/caitlin-johnstone-unprovoked/

118. Johnstone, C. (2024, December 17). Australia Unveils Plan To Fight 'Antisemitism' By Crushing Free Speech. Caitlin's Newsletter. https://www.caitlinjohnst.one/p/australia-unveils-plan-to-fight-antisemitism

119. Justice Law (Google Translate, Trans.). (1993, December 31). Enlace Zapatista. https://enlacezapatista.ezln.org.mx/1993/12/31/ley-de-justicia/

120. Kenyon, G. (2020, July 2). Aboriginal protesters defend forest against loggers. Dw.Com. https://www.dw.com/en/australia-aboriginal-protesters-defend-ancient-forest-against-logging/a-53979480

121. Khan, M. (2019, August 28). Islam and Four Essential Freedoms. Maydan. https://themaydan.com/2019/08/islam-and-four-essential-freedoms/

122. Khatib, R., McKee, M., & Yusuf, S. (2024). Counting the dead in Gaza: Difficult but essential. The Lancet, 404(10449), 237–238. https://doi.org/10.1016/S0140-6736(24)01169-3

123. Kim, S. J. (2025, April 5). JESUS DIED FOR OUR SINS AND WAS RISEN. UBF: University Bible Fellowship. https://www.ubf.org/resources/show/jesus-died-for-our-sins-and-was-risen

Kimmerer, R. (2013). Braiding Sweetgrass. Milkweed Editions.

124. Chapter "A Mother's Work"

125. Chapter "Allegiance to Gratitude"

126. Chapter "Putting Down Roots"

127. Chapter "Skywoman Falling"

128. Chapter "The Gift of Strawberries"

129. Chapter "The Three Sisters"

130. Chapter "Windigo Footprints"

131. Chapter "Wisgaak Gokpenagen: A Black Ash Basket"

King James Version Bible. (n.d.).

132. 1 Corinthians 11:3

133. Luke 23:2

134. Mark 11:15-18

135. Mark 9:31

136. King Jr, M. L. (1963, April 16). Letter from Birmingham Jail. https://letterfromjail.com/

137. King Jr, M. L. (1967, April 4). Beyond Vietnam: A Time to Break Silence. World Future Fund. https://www.worldfuturefund.org/Reports2013/Martinlutherkingspeech1967.html

138. King Jr, M. L. (1968, April 3). I've Been to the Mountaintop. https://www.afscme.org/about/history/mlk/mountaintop

139. Kirk, J. (2020, August 10). Martin Luther King Jr. New Georgia Encyclopedia. https://www.georgiaencyclopedia.org/articles/arts-culture/martin-luther-king-jr-1929-1968/

140. Koch Industries: Secretly Funding the Climate Denial Machine. (2024, August 4). Greenpeace. https://www.greenpeace.org/usa/climate/climate-deniers/koch-industries/

Koehler, J. (1999). Stasi: The Untold Story of the East German Secret Police. Westview Press.

141. Chapter "The Sword of Repression"

142. kswheeler. (2011, September 8). This Day in Resistance History: Sitting Bull's Railway Speech. Grand Rapids Institute for Information Democracy. https://griid.org/2011/09/08/this-day-in-resistance-history-sitting-bull%e2%80%99s-railway-speech/

Landon, P. (1905). Lhasa (Vol. 1). Hurst and Blackett, Ltd.

143. p. 350

144. Law on the Rights and Obligations of Peoples in Struggle (Google Translate, Trans.). (1993, December 31). Enlace Zapatista. https://enlacezapatista.ezln.org.mx/1993/12/31/ley-de-derechos-y-obligaciones-de-los-pueblos-en-lucha/

145. Laybourn, K. (2022, August 17). UK strikes: How Margaret Thatcher and other leaders cut trade union powers over centuries. The Conversation. http://theconversation.com/uk-strikes-how-margaret-thatcher-and-other-leaders-cut-trade-union-powers-over-centuries-186420

146. Ley Revolucionaria de Mujeres. (1993, December 31). Enlace Zapatista. https://enlacezapatista.ezln.org.mx/1993/12/31/ley-revolucionaria-de-mujeres/

Liedloff, J. (2004). The Continuum Concept. Penguin Group.

147. Chapter "Growing Up"

Linderman, F. (1932). Red Mother. The John Day Company.

148. p. 173   **149.** p. 21   **150.** p. 22

151. p. 84

152. Lockheed Martin Board Elects James D. Taiclet as Chairman; Marillyn A. Hewson to Serve as Strategic Advisor and Gregory M. Ulmer as Executive Vice President of Aeronautics. (2021, January 29). Lockheed Martin. https://news.lockheedmartin.com/2021-01-29-Lockheed-Martin-Board-Elects-James-D-Taiclet-as-Chairman-Marillyn-A-Hewson-to-Serve-as-Strategic-Advisor-and-Gregory-M-Ulmer-as-Executive-Vice-President-of-Aeronautics

Loewen, J. (2007). Lies My Teacher Told Me. The New Press.

153. p. 107   **154.** p. 108

155. Lohnes, K. (2024, May 21). Siege of Jerusalem. Encyclopedia Britannica. https://www.britannica.com/event/Siege-of-Jerusalem-70

156. MacQueen, G. (2006, August). 156 Eyewitnesses Whose Statements Are Suggestive Of Explosions In The Twin Towers. ae911truth.org. https://www1.ae911truth.org/downloads/156eyewitnessaccounts.pdf

157. Mahdavi, D. (2023, April 6). New study indicates chemicals from grocery stickers may be leaching into foods. Here's what you need to know. CBC News. https://www.cbc.ca/news/canada/kitchener-waterloo/bps-food-labels-1.6792373

158. Maimann, K. (2025, February 13). '1.7 million' Palestinians in Gaza? Trump's statement raises questions about death toll | CBC News. CBC. https://www.cbc.ca/news/world/trump-gaza-population-relocation-1.7457559

159. Malinowski, S., Sheets, A., & Schmittroth, L. (Eds.). (1999). UXL Encyclopedia of Native American Tribes (Vol. 1). UXL.

Mantell, D. (1974). True Americanism. Teachers College Press.

160. p. 137   **161.** p. 141   **162.** p. 147

163. p. 151   **164.** p. 25   **165.** p. 27

166. p. 3   **167.** p. 50

168. Marcetic, B. (2024, May 24). Evidence Is Mounting That the Saudis Had a Hand in 9/11. Jacobin. https://jacobin.com/2024/05/saudi-arabia-9-11-al-bayoumi-revelations

169. Marcos. (1994, January 4). Subcomandante Marcos: We have been preparing in the mountains for ten years. Enlace Zapatista. https://enlacezapatista.ezln.org.mx/1994/01/04/subcomandante-marcos-nos-hemos-estado-preparando-en-la-montana-desde-hace-diez-anos/

170. Marcos, S. (2014, July 22). The Zapatista Women's Revolutionary Law as it is lived today. Open Democracy. https://www.opendemocracy.net/en/zapatista-womens-revolutionary-law-as-it-is-lived-today/

171. Maté, A. (2022, March 5). By using Ukraine to fight Russia, the US provoked Putin's war. Aaronmate.Net. https://www.aaronmate.net/p/by-using-ukraine-to-fight-russia

172. Matthews, L. (2020, April 6). Nonstick Pans and Forever Chemicals: What You Need to Know. LeafScore. https://www.leafscore.com/eco-friendly-kitchen-products/the-problem-with-teflon-and-other-non-stick-pots-and-pans/

173. McCormick, M. (2025, August 7). The Obedience and Sinlessness of Christ. The Gospel Coalition. https://www.thegospelcoalition.org/essay/obedience-sinlessness-christ/

174. Meir, N. (2020, June 19). The decision to capitalize Black. AP. https://www.ap.org/the-definitive-source/announcements/the-decision-to-capitalize-black/

175. Messiah. (2024, August 20). Oxford Reference. https://www.oxfordreference.com/display/10.1093/oi/authority.20110803100152530

176. Miller, R. (2015). American Indian Constitutions and Their Influence on the United States Constitution. Proceedings of the American Philosophical Society, 159(1). https://ssrn.com/abstract=2739936

177. Morgan, T. (2018, March 22). The NRA Supported Gun Control When the Black Panthers Had the Weapons. HISTORY. https://www.history.com/articles/black-panthers-gun-control-nra-support-mulford-act

178. Mujeres 45% de las bases zapatistas. (2011, November 30). Cimacnoticias.Com.Mx. https://cimacnoticias.com.mx/2003/11/19/mujeres-45-de-las-bases-zapatistas/

179. Myers, I. (2025, March 18). EWG's Dirty Dozen Guide to Food Chemicals: The top 12 to avoid | Environmental Working Group. EWG. https://www.ewg.org/consumer-guides/ewgs-dirty-dozen-guide-food-chemicals-top-12-avoid

180. Nawawi. (2025, August 7). 40HadithNawawi: Hadith 13. 40HadithNawawi. https://40hadithnawawi.com/hadith/13-love-for-your-brother-what-you-love-for-yourself

Neihardt, J. (2014). Black Elk Speaks. University of Nebraska Press.

181. Chapter "Footnotes"

Nelson, M. (Ed.). (2008). Original Instructions. Bear and Company.

182. Chapter "A Democracy Based On Peace"   **183.** Chapter "An Okanagan World view of Society"   **184.** Chapter "Definition of Indigenous Knowledge"

185. Chapter "Ethiopian Women: From Passive Resources to Active Citizens"   **186.** Chapter "First Nations Survival and the Future of the Earth"   **187.** Chapter "Peace Technologies from the San Bushmen of Africa"

188. Chapter "Return of the Ancient Council Ways: Indigenous Survival in Chiapas"

189. Nelson, S. (2023, May 24). IRS opened probe into Matt Taibbi's taxes after Twitter dump. New York Post. https://nypost.com/2023/05/24/irs-opened-probe-into-matt-taibbis-taxes-after-twitter-dump/

New International Version Bible. (n.d.).

190. 1 Peter 2:13
191. 1 Peter 2:16
192. Luke 6:31
193. Mark 10:32-34
194. Mark 12:17
195. Mark 2:27
196. Mark 3:2
197. Matthew 12:10
198. Matthew 4:1-11

199. Ninth Part: The new structure of Zapastista Autonomy (Google Translate, Trans.). (2023, November 14). Enlace Zapatista. https://enlacezapatista.ezln.org.mx/2023/11/13/ninth-part-the-new-structure-of-zapastista-autonomy/

200. North Carolina Lawmakers Approve Mask Bill That Allows Health Exemption After Pushback. (2024, June 11). US News & World Report. http://www.usnews.com/news/best-states/north-carolina/articles/2024-06-11/north-carolina-lawmakers-approve-mask-bill-that-allows-health-exemption-after-pushback

Notes, A. (Ed.). (2005). Basic Call To Consciousness. Native Voices.

201. p. 104
202. p. 105
203. p. 114
204. p. 34
205. p. 35
206. p. 37
207. p. 38
208. p. 39
209. p. 49

210. Offenhartz, J. (2025, March 9). ICE arrests Palestinian activist Mahmoud Khalil. AP. https://apnews.com/article/columbia-university-mahmoud-khalil-ice-15014bcbb921f21a9f704d5acdcae7a8

Olsen, O. (1962). The Ku Klux Klan: A Study in Reconstruction Politics and Propaganda. North Carolina Office of Archives and History, 39(3).

211. pp. 353-354

212. Padierna Jiménez, M. del P. (2013). Mujeres Zapatistas: La inclusión de las demandas de género. Argumentos (México, D.F.), 26(73), 133–142.

213. PCBS | The International Population Day, 11/07/2023. (2025, August 6). Palestinian Central Bureau of Statistics. https://www.pcbs.gov.ps/post.aspx?lang=en&ItemID=4544

214. Perla, S. (2022, September 15). Obedience: Virtue and Counsel. The Catholic Project. https://catholicproject.catholic.edu/obedience-virtue-and-counsel/

215. Peter, L., & Vock, I. (2023, October 12). French police break up pro-Palestinian demo after ban. https://www.bbc.com/news/world-europe-67088567

Pharr, C. (Ed.). (1952). Book XVI 1.2. In The Theodosian Code. Princeton University Press.

216. p. 440

Prechtel, M. (1999). Secrets of the Talking Jaguar. Tarcher.

217. p. 111
218. p. 202
219. p. 209
220. p. 210
221. p. 275
222. pp. 99-100

223. Prescott, J. (1975). Body Pleasure and the Origins of Violence. The Bulletin of The Atomic Scientists, 10–20.

224. Prescott, J. (1977). Child Abuse in America: Slaughter of the Innocents. Hustler. https://www.violence.de/prescott/hustler-new/article.html

Price, W. (2002). Nutrition and Physical Degeneration. Project Gutenberg of Australia.

225. Chapter "Physical, Mental, and Moral Degeneration"

Randolph, W. (2024). One Disease One Cure: Ending Our Multi-Millennia Catastrophe. Three Integrities Publishing. https://1disease-1cure.com/

226. "Chapter 10 - Profit Economies"
227. "Chapter 20: Imposing And Maintaining Racism vs Generating Unity"
228. "Chapter 22: Imposing And Maintaining Hatred"
229. "Chapter 24: Sexual Discrimination vs Sexual Equality"
230. "Chapter 25: Sexual Freedom vs Sexual Repression"
231. "Chapter 32: A Study in Privilege and World-Shaping - the Police"
232. "Chapter 36: Sabotaging Efforts at Deep Cultural Healing"
233. "Chapter 40: Enough! - The Zapatistas' Deep Revolution"
234. "Chapter 47: Embracing the Sacred Masculine"
235. "Chapter 6: Blind Belief 1 - When People Ignore Reality to Maintain Safety and Comfort"

236. Rebecca Liebert. (2024, July 15). Lubrizol. https://www.lubrizol.com/Our-Company/CEO-and-Leadership/Leadership/Rebecca-Liebert

237. Revolutionary Agriculture Law (Google Translate, Trans.). (1993, December 31). Enlace Zapatista. https://enlacezapatista.ezln.org.mx/1993/12/31/ley-agraria-revolucionaria/

Rockhill, W. W. (1892). Udanavarga: A Collection of Verses from the Buddhist Canon. Routledge.

238. p. 252

239. Rodríguez, S. (1994, March 8). Comandanta Ramona y Mayor Ana María: Las demandas son las mismas de siempre: Justicia, tierras, trabajo, educación e igualdad para las mujeres. Enlace Zapatista. https://enlacezapatista.ezln.org.mx/1994/03/07/comandanta-ramona-y-mayor-ana-maria-las-demandas-son-las-mismas-de-siempre-justicia-tierras-trabajo-educacion-e-igualdad-para-las-mujeres/

Rong, J. (2008). Wolf Totem (H. Goldblatt, Trans.). Penguin Press.

240. "Chapter 2"

241. Rull, M. R. (2021, August 2). In the face of assassinations and paramilitary terror, the Zapatista struggle for sovereignty continues. War Resisters. https://wagingnonviolence.org/wr/2021/08/assassinations-paramilitary-terror-zapatista-struggle-sovereignty/

242. Russia: Sakhalin Island indigenous peoples protest oil development. (2005, January 31). Cultural Survival. https://www.culturalsurvival.org/news/russia-sakhalin-island-indigenous-peoples-protest-oil-development

Ryan, C., & Jethá, C. (2010). Sex at Dawn. HarperCollins.

243. "Chapter 9: Paternity Certainty: The Crumbling Cornerstone of the Standard Narrative"

244. Satter, D. (2016, August 15). The Bloody Czar. National Review. https://www.nationalreview.com/magazine/2016/08/15/vladimir-putin-presidency-russian-terrorism/

245. Scahill, J. (2024, February 7). Netanyahu's War on Truth. The Intercept. https://theintercept.com/2024/02/07/gaza-israel-netanyahu-propaganda-lies-palestinians/

246. Sharp, J. (2025). U.S. Foreign Aid to Israel: Overview and Developments since October 7, 2023. Congressional Research Service. https://www.congress.gov/crs_external_products/RL/PDF/RL33222/RL33222.51.pdf

247. Sirota, D., & Perez, A. (2015, May 26). Weapons Deals And The Clinton Foundation. International Business Times. https://www.ibtimes.com/clinton-foundation-donors-got-weapons-deals-hillary-clintons-state-department-1934187

248. Skerk, J. (2022, September 29). Rural Europe Takes Action | The Sámi Environmental Programme. Resilience. https://www.resilience.org/stories/2022-09-29/rural-europe-takes-action-the-sami-environmental-programme/

249. Sloan, G. (2020, August 30). DC: Police Violently Push Protesters From Black Lives Matter. Associated Press. https://newsroom.ap.org/editorial-photos-videos/detail?itemid=8a49947717c1441e9ad149e1c2d8faa6&mediatype=photo

Smith, J. (2016). The Dame Janet Smith Review Report. https://downloads.bbci.co.uk/bbctrust/assets/files/pdf/our_work/dame_janet_smith_review/conclusions_summaries.pdf

250. pp. 3-4   **251.** p. 49

252. Solidarity protests with Palestinian people banned in at least 12 EU countries. (2024, April 24). Civicus. https://viewer.mapme.com/875ac156-c9a9-4664-a26a-fca8e96d0260

253. Solomon, E. (2024, September 23). Israeli-Arab Girl, 12, Suspended From School After Empathizing With G.... Haaretz. https://www.haaretz.com/israel-news/2024-09-24/ty-article/.premium/israeli-arab-girl-12-suspended-from-school-after-empathizing-with-gazan-children/00000192-20a6-dc44-affb-39fb8a800000

254. Solon, P. (2017, December 8). TIPNIS: The Saga for the Rights of Nature and Indigenous People. CounterPunch.Org. https://www.counterpunch.org/2017/12/08/tipnis-the-saga-for-the-rights-of-nature-and-indigenous-people/

255. Standing Rock Sioux Reservation. (2024, August 2). Sitting Bull College. https://sittingbull.edu/about/community/visitor-center/standing-rock-sioux-tribe/

256. Stapley, D. (1977, October 1). The Blessings of Righteous Obedience. The Church of Jesus Christ of Latter-Day Saints. https://www.churchofjesuschrist.org/study/eng/general-conference/1977/10/the-blessings-of-righteous-obedience

Strong, A. L. (1976). When Serfs Stood Up In Tibet. Red Sun Publishers.

257. p. 329

258. Stuchbery, M. (2019, December 18). Why Germany will never forget the Stasi era of mass surveillance—Th.... The Local. https://www.thelocal.de/20190208/what-the-stasi-show-about-an-unforgotten-era-of-mass-surveillance

259. Tapped out: America's drinking water and the health risks hidden behind legal limits. (2025, February). EWG. https://www.ewg.org/tapwater/state-of-american-drinking-water.php

260. Taylor-Neu, R., Friedel, T., Taylor, A., & Kemble, T. (2018). (De)Constructing The 'Lazy Indian': An Historical Analysis of Welfare Reform in Canada. Aboriginal Policy Studies, 7(2). https://doi.org/10.5663/aps.v7i2.29340

261. Team Vice. (2022, February 14). What Do Australia's Coal Miners Think of Climate Change? VICE. https://www.vice.com/en/article/what-do-australias-coal-miners-think-of-climate-change/

262. The Black Panther Party. (2025, August 5). Mutual Aid. https://www.mutualaid.coop/history/black-panther-party/

263. The Editors of the Encyclopedia Britannica. (2024a, June 21). Utopia. https://www.britannica.com/topic/utopia

264. The Editors of the Encyclopedia Britannica. (2024b, August 5). John J. McCloy. Encyclopedia Britannica. https://www.britannica.com/biography/John-J-McCloy

265. The First Discourse of the Buddha. (2024, July 21). Vipassana Research Institute. https://www.vridhamma.org/discourses/first-discourse-of-buddha

266. The global scale of child sexual abuse in the Catholic Church. (2021, October 5). Al Jazeera. https://www.aljazeera.com/news/2021/10/5/awful-truth-child-sex-abuse-in-the-catholic-church

The Quran (M. Khattab, Trans.). (n.d.).

267. Verse 2:216   **268.** Verse 2:220   **269.** Verse 2:224
270. Verse 4:34   **271.** Verse 4:59

Thoreau, H. D. (2021). Walden. Project Gutenberg. https://www.gutenberg.org/files/205/205-h/205-h.htm

272. Chapter "Economy"

Tims, F., & Ludford, J. (Eds.). (1983). Drug Abuse Treatment Evaluation: Strategies, Progress, and Prospects. Department of Health and Human Services, Public Health Service, Alcohol, Drug Abuse, and Mental Health Administration. https://archives.nida.nih.gov/sites/default/files/monograph51.pdf

273. p. 3

274. Tremlett, G. (2002, November 27). Portugal's elite linked to paedophile ring. The Guardian. https://www.theguardian.com/world/2002/nov/27/childprotection.uk

275. Tremlett, G. (2010, September 3). Carlos Cruz sentenced to seven years for paedophile offences. The Guardian. https://www.theguardian.com/world/2010/sep/03/portugal-paedophile-ring

Trigger, B. (1969). The Huron Farmers of the North. Holt, Rinehart and Winston.

276. p. 26 **277.** p. 40 **278.** p. 44

279. p. 71

280. Trudeau, J. (2022, December 10). Statement by the Prime Minister on Human Rights Day. Prime Minister of Canada. https://www.pm.gc.ca/en/news/statements/2022/12/10/statement-prime-minister-human-rights-day

Tsering, T., Goldstein, M., & Siebenschuh, W. (1997). The Struggle for Modern Tibet. ME Sharpe, Inc.

281. "Chapter 3"

Turner, F. (1994). Beyond Geography. Rutgers University Press.

282. Chapter "Possession"

283. Unger, C. (2018, December 4). Bush's sordid Saudi ties set template for Trump – he was just more subtle. The Guardian. https://www.theguardian.com/us-news/2018/dec/04/george-hw-bush-saudi-arabia-donald-trump

284. Urban Reform Law (Google Translate, Trans.). (1993, December 31). Enlace Zapatista. https://enlacezapatista.ezln.org.mx/1993/12/31/ley-de-reforma-urbana/

285. Vasili Arkhipov: The Unsung Hero Who Saved the World from Nuclear Annihilation. (2024, May 26). History Tools. https://www.historytools.org/stories/vasili-arkhipov-the-unsung-hero-who-saved-the-world-from-nuclear-annihilation

Vestal, S. (with Grinnell, G.). (1955). The Fighting Cheyennes. University of Oklahoma Press.

286. Chapter "Introduction"

287. Volkow, N. (2021, June 8). Addiction Should Be Treated, Not Penalized. NIMHD Insights. https://blog.nimhd.nih.gov/archives-2021/news_feed/addiction-should-be-treated-not-penalized

288. Wall Street's Ongoing Crime Spree. (2022). Better Markets. https://bettermarkets.org/wp-content/uploads/2022/05/BetterMarkets_Wall_Street_RAP_Sheet_Report_052022.pdf

289. War is Boring. (2014, July 8). The U.S. Names Lots of Weapons After Native Americans. Medium. https://medium.com/war-is-boring/twenty-u-s-weapons-named-after-native-americans-8b88e2c7ed12

290. Weiss, I. (2024, May 26). Kevin O'Leary's dystopian fantasy of ruining the lives of campus protesters. The Hill. https://thehill.com/opinion/technology/4686937-kevin-olearys-dystopian-fantasy-of-ruining-the-lives-of-campus-protesters/

291. Weiss, K. (2009). Boys Will Be Boys. Violence Against Women, 15(7). https://doi.org/10.1177/1077801209333611

292. Weston, J. (2017, March 3). Water is Life: The Rise of the Mní Wičóni Movement. Cultural Survival. https://www.culturalsurvival.org/publications/cultural-survival-quarterly/water-life-rise-mni-wiconi-movement

293. Wimpee, R. (2020, November 4). Funding a Social Movement: The Ford Foundation and Civil Rights, 1965-1970. RE:Source. https://resource.rockarch.org/story/philanthropy-social-movements-ford-foundation-civil-rights-1965-1970/

Wood, C. (with Fee, C.). (1936). Chief Joseph The Biography of a Great Indian. Wilson-Erickson.

294. p. 336

Young, J. (n.d.-a). Kamana Three: Nature Awareness Trail (M. Wild, L. Cunio, & D. Gardoqui, Eds.; Vol. 3). Owlink Media.

295. p. 14 **296.** p. 15

Young, J. (n.d.-b). Kamana Two: Nature Awareness Trail (M. Wild & L. Cunio, Eds.; Vol. 2). Owlink Media.

297. p. 1 **298.** p. 7 **299.** p. ix

300. Zituni, D. (2024, May 24). New Report Analyzes Crackdown on Palestine Solidarity in the U.S. Palestine Legal. https://palestinelegal.org/news/2024/5/23/new-report-analyzes-crackdown-on-palestine-solidarity-in-the-usnbsp

www.ingramcontent.com/pod-product-compliance
Lightning Source LLC
Chambersburg PA
CBHW060750050426
42449CB00008B/1342